Opening the *Aloha* Mind

Healing Self,
Healing the World
with
Ho'oponopono

Jim Nourse, PhD

BALBOA.
PRESS
A DIVISION OF HAY HOUSE

Balboa Press books may be ordered through booksellers or by contacting:

Balboa Press
A Division of Hay House
1663 Liberty Drive
Bloomington, IN 47403
www.balboapress.com
1-(877) 407-4847

Printed in the United States of America.

ISBN: 978-1-4525-8100-2 (sc)
ISBN: 978-1-4525-8102-6 (hc)
ISBN: 978-1-4525-8101-9 (e)

Library of Congress Control Number: 2013915494

Balboa Press rev. date: 12/11/2013

Clean, erase, erase,
And create your own Shangri La
Where? Within yourself!

—*Morrnah Nalamaku Simeona*

To Kopa
Me Ke Aloha Pumehana

ACKNOWLEDGEMENTS

I have been greatly blessed with wonderful teachers in this life. Special thanks to Dan Austin, Stan and Christina Grof, Michael Harner, Beautiful Painted Arrow, Jack Kornfield, Pannadipa and Pannavati.

Mahalo nui loa to Dr. 'Ihaleakalā Hew Len for his clarity, wisdom and humor in spreading the liberating message of Self I-dentity Through Ho'oponopono® and to Morrnah Nalamaku Simeona for her inspired re-visioning of the ancient practice.

A special mahalo to Stanley Kopa Kaluahine, Kahuna Lapa'au and dear friend who continues to show us the meaning of the Aloha Spirit.

Love and gratitude to our friends Joshua, Annaleah and Valerie, who help us stay connected with Paradise.

I greatly appreciate my editor, David Colin Carr, who not only rendered a clean manuscript but also really understood this subject and its importance for our time. David's nurturance of this project's unfolding has far exceeded the formal task of editing.

And thanks be to my best friend, soul companion, wife, and ipo Judith. We'll travel somewhere other than Hawai'i . . . soon . . . I promise.

TABLE OF CONTENTS

A BRIEF NOTE ABOUT FORMAT

Throughout this book, a blank page will occur between the ending of one chapter and the beginning of the next. This convention is included as a symbol of *returning to Zero*, the heart of the process you are about to discover. It is also an invitation to see the blank pages as the real subject of this book.

This energy, this tapestry of aloha, is the most powerful of all the forces in the universe. And only when you are in the state of aloha, only then you can truly touch the universe.

Kahuna Hale Kealohalani Makua

from *The Bowl of Light* by Hank Wesselman

INTRODUCTION

What follows is a labor of love and at the same time a journey cautiously undertaken out of conviction. I have seen the process it describes impact both my clients and my personal life. I have grown to trust that there is a level of healing wisdom which the ancient world knew well, but which modern medicine and psychology access only by accident, if at all. This book is a labor of love that is riding a cultural wave which is rising to restore balance to a world view and philosophy of healing that has become one-sided in excluding so much of what is essential to true healing.

The caution I feel in adding my understanding to this philosophy and the methods that emerge from it is twofold. First, a technique may be mastered after a few repetitions, but mastering the mindset in which it is embedded and enables it to be used with true comprehension, is an evolving art. Accompanying this is the unconscious resistance to novelty. While we may wish to know something new, the old can have formidable inertia. True understanding consists not just of what we have learned but of what we have been willing to unlearn.

For the seasoned teacher and practitioner of this approach, this book will hopefully be patiently regarded as devoted effort of one who has much to unlearn to come to grips with a method that has pleased his heart while challenging his burdensome intellect—which makes this an opportunity for all of us to practice the process.

The second caution I confront is my awareness that the world's native peoples have been exploited enough. Land has been taken, religion replaced, native language forbidden to be taught to the children. Their civilization lays waste, and now, in our own emptiness and restlessness, we return for a taste of that spirituality our forebears did their best to destroy. Today as my wife and I left the company of our Hawaiian friend and teacher, I was stopped by a wave of grief that seemed to come up from the ground through my feet. It felt like the crying of many souls, and of the land. It felt both current and very old.

A shaman we know came under fire from some in his tribal family who felt that white people did not deserve access to the sacred knowledge. Enough has been taken already, they implored. Do not give them what is closest to our heart and spirit. He conceded that much had been stolen, but the question is no longer of deserving. With the world so perilously close to the edge of an abyss, there is no choice but to teach all who are willing to learn, those who seek sanity, so the world may have a chance.

The efforts of a suppressed people to awaken to and take pride in their unique cultural and spiritual identity naturally creates an aversion to outsiders laying claim to their wisdom. Yet the discovery of sublime value in these ideas, I believe, is not an insult, but an honor. These ideas are not static remnants of a forgotten time, but living truths that are an offering to a larger world in great need of them. Will this knowledge change the world? Hopefully. Will it be changed by the world? That is how the collective consciousness of humanity evolves. If my part in this process has offended any native person, I humbly ask for forgiveness. At the same time, I offer my deepest gratitude and trust that we are moving, however fitfully, toward a world in which we all live from the foundation of our shared Self I-dentity.

I have learned many methods in the course of my career as a psychologist, yet this one not only fascinates me, but perplexes me with its sense of urgency to be shared. No other approach has aroused such feelings of being inadequate to the task nor being the right person for it. Training as a psychologist is not entirely irrelevant to this venture, but it is not a qualification.

The decision to proceed with the writing and, ultimately, with the publication of this book is the result of ongoing practice of the process it describes. In the grip of conflicting ideas and feelings, it is often impossible to think one's way to clarity. Wisdom counsels not only waiting for clarity, but calling upon that faculty of mind that sees beyond the inner debate—a faculty that can clean the mind of the arguments that paralyze it. This book is about achieving that clarity and moving toward an experience of peace that is inherently contagious.

With gratitude and Aloha,
James C. Nourse, Ph.D., L.Ac.
Kapaʻa, Kauaʻi
January 14, 2010

What you were feeling was the spiritual power of the island, what we call mana.

Kahuna Stanley Kopa Kaluahine

CHAPTER ONE

A Taste of Mana

> . . . the human beings (Native Americans), my son,
> they believe everything is alive.
> Not only man and animals. But also water, earth, stone.

> Grandfather Old Lodge Skins
> in *Little Big Man*

This book is about a philosophy, a technique, a process called Self I-dentity Through Ho'oponopono®—simply referred to hereinafter as Ho'oponopono. This term traditionally refers to an ancient Polynesian system of conflict resolution and forgiveness. Here, Ho'oponopono refers to an inner process that is a natural development from its historical predecessor.

It is, first and foremost, a problem-solving strategy. What distinguishes it from most other such strategies is that it seeks to solve problems by working on oneself rather than on external circumstances. When using

1

Ho'oponopono, one finds that, as the self is brought into a state of balance and clarity, the external world is experienced as less problematic. In fact, problems are seen as opportunities to achieve greater balance and clarity. In addition, the ongoing practice of Ho'oponopono can lead to a more harmonious experience of life, and the knowledge that one's happiness is not dependent upon external events.

While this subject can stand on its own, for me its beauty and richness are enhanced by reference to history and cultural context. Our modern western mindset reduces our healing interventions to the "active ingredient." Yet, that ingredient in an herbal medicine, when extracted, synthesized and concentrated, brings daunting side effects in the absence of buffering influences supplied by the "inactive" rejected plant components. So historical and cultural factors surrounding a practice add to a person's ability to assimilate it so it is no longer merely one more technique in the repertoire.

I trust that learning some things about the soil from which Ho'oponopono springs will also help you appreciate its beauty as well as its utility. I believe you will come to see that, while Ho'oponopono is thoroughly Hawaiian, it carries a universal resonance that is needed to achieve a complete understanding of our human nature and, in turn, achieve healing and wholeness.

From Kaua'i to the Big Island of Hawai'i, Hawai'i is a land that is at once ancient and newly forming. As the lava of Kīlauea volcano flows into the sea, cooling and solidifying into new land, the ancient teachings are at the same time flowing into new forms and new expressions.

The psychospiritual teachings of Hawai'i express the collective experience of a tropical island civilization and carry the spirit of this particular land and people. While the beauty and profundity of the teachings may be seen as unique facets of this beautiful land, their ultimate value is that they have tapped universal principles embedded deeply within human nature itself. These principles address the structure of mind, its relation to the Divine, and knowing how to use the energy that powers this structure to evoke internal freedom and healing.

Anyone who is open to the people of these islands soon learns that sovereignty is a big issue. Statehood was not welcomed by consensus, and there is lingering resentment concerning the overthrow of the monarchy in 1893 and the annexation by the U.S. in 1898. While political issues are peripheral to the heart of this book, the desire of all people to be free, independent and self-determining is not. Just as the Hawaiian nation might find its fullest expression free of foreign domination, so individual human beings can find fullest expression freed from the domination of deeply imprinted thoughts, attitudes and beliefs that hide their true identity and highest potential. In a very real sense, we are all colonized people. We all struggle against powers that seem to dominate us—addictions, worry, self-defeating behavior, depression, disease, or other afflictions that overrun us with regularity and persistence, so that we often cast ourselves as victims, rather than the heroes in our own stories. The quest for personal sovereignty is, in a very real sense, the central sacred task of each person. A psychologically sovereign individual is comfortable in her own skin—self-assured yet flexible, at ease with change, and able to participate in the affairs of family and community in a way that benefits all.

The challenge is how to lay the groundwork for such a sublime state of being. Often, our desire to pursue it begins with a spontaneous and unexpected experience. I had never had any particular interest in Hawai'i, but in 1999 my wife Judith attended a professional conference in Honolulu and I went along. I spent the days driving around O'ahu.

Leaving Waikīkī on the first day, I headed windward on the Pali Highway and pulled off on a spur road with a view of stunning green cliffs descending to the ocean. When I was a very young child I used to play, over and over again, a 78 rpm recording of *South Pacific* in which

Juanita Hall sang *Bali Hai*. This haunting melody resurfaced in my mind with all its original magic upon encountering this remarkable visage just minutes outside Honolulu. After lingering awhile and allowing myself to begin to ease in to these powerful new surroundings, I then proceeded north on Kamehameha Highway, named after the ali'i (chief) who united the islands under one rule in 1810. After passing through the city of Kāne'ohe the scenery steadily merged into more rural stretches with blue-green ocean to the right and verdant mountains to the left, reflecting the long process of island-building by the central volcano. O'ahu actually consists of two such volcanic ridges, whose ancient lava flows merge into a central valley.

I began to enter an extraordinary state of mind, a sense of profound well-being that was clearly more than a sense of pleasure in the beautiful scenery or the relaxation associated with being on vacation. It was paradoxically ecstatic and serene at the same time. My internal being and the external environment seemed in resonance, an energy that felt loving, welcoming and powerful. This remarkable state persisted throughout the remainder of the day and beyond.

Later, in attempting to understand this experience, my reading led me to the Hawaiian notion of *mana*. Mana is supernatural energy or spiritual power contained and expressed by objects both animate and inanimate. People of outstanding ability or mastery in any field are thought to possess more mana than the ordinary person. It did not seem to me to be a far stretch to think that certain geographic locations could be regions of abundant mana, and that this might account for my experience of heightened awareness.

Our next trip to Hawai'i included a visit to Kaua'i, geologically the oldest of the eight main Hawaiian islands. On our first full day there we went to the Hikina A Ka Lā Heiau and adjacent Hauola City of Refuge. A heiau is a place of worship that served the indigenous religion. There are many heiau still standing. Most were abandoned with the dissolution of the old religion and what remain are often arrangements of volcanic boulders that give an impression of the contours of an ancient structure. These sacred sites suffered along with the rest of Hawaiian culture as foreign influences came to dominate the islands. The reawakening of native Hawaiian consciousness is restoring respect for the ancient practices, sites and institutions such that now the heiau are once again accorded the sacred status they deserve.

Judith and I felt moved to spend some time in silent meditation at this heiau and when we were finished we were approached by a Hawaiian man wearing sunglasses and a feathered hat. Because his eyes were invisible, I wasn't altogether sure of our situation. Had we angered him by unintentionally violating a sacred protocol? He said "I see you guys are hangin' out at the heaiu." I replied "Yes, we were meditating here. I hope that's OK." "Ohhh, that's good!" he responded. He then introduced himself as Kopa Kaluahine, a spiritual healing practitioner on the island. Further experience affirmed him to be a Kahuna Lapaʻau, an individual who had achieved a high level of mastery in this field, having been trained initially by his grandmother. We struck up a friendship that has continued to this day.

At one point the conversation turned to the subject of mana. He suggested that the unusual experience we had had from our first visit to Oʻahu was that of the mana of the islands. He allowed that, for him, the mana of Kauaʻi is stronger than that of any of the other islands, and having been to several of the others, I had to agree that this seemed true for me also. Whether the individual's experience of the mana is purely a function of the island itself or of one's connection to a particular island is unclear to me. "People have their own feelings about one island or another. For me, the connection to Kauaʻi is stronger," he noted. One of his gifts to us was a Pōhaku, or stone, that he had used in his healing work. He had invested the Pōhaku with some of his mana so that we could make use of it in our own healing practices back on the mainland.

The combination of a clear and powerful experience of the mana of the islands, with its linkage to the activity and vocation of healing via our Kahuna friend, formed the character of our introduction to Hawai'i. It also cued my attention to any practice that owes its origins to this remote archipelago. As a transpersonal psychologist I am naturally drawn to investigate any approach that has not artificially separated the psyche from the spirit, and the fact that a contemporary practice can legitimately claim ancient origins suggests a track record to be taken seriously.

My remarkable taste of mana on O'ahu and Kaua'i—including a sublime resonance between self and environment—is characteristic of being at ease, "in synch" or "in the flow." The fact that such an experience *can* happen indicates that we are equipped for it *to* happen—given the right conditions of specific environments or circumstances. While my own experience suggests that the particular mana of a given geography is supportive, if we limit our thinking to this sort of contingency, we are ironically setting a trap of dependency on external conditions of place and time in order to experience peace and happiness.

Perhaps the ultimate value of extraordinary experiences is to acquaint us with the fact that it is within our potential as human beings to be in a state of real connection with ourselves and our world, and that this may, in fact be our natural state. Once we have tasted such an experience, our assignment naturally becomes how to configure *ourselves* to remain in this state of flow regardless of where we are or with whom. This is true sovereignty and true freedom—and is the import of what will unfold in these pages.

One should lie empty, open, choiceless as a beach—waiting for a gift from the sea.

Anne Morrow Lindbergh

CHAPTER TWO

It's A Beautiful Day

To see a world in a grain of sand
And heaven in a wild flower
Hold infinity in the palm of your hand
And eternity in an hour

William Blake
Auguries of Innocence

Our friend Joshua shifted the Nissan pickup into 4WD as we pulled onto what loosely passed for a road leading away from Polihale beach. For several days rain had pelted the island, even on the usually dry leeward side. The storm system hovering just off the north shore was stretching around to the margins of the southernmost pali (cliffs) that form the northern reach of Polihale. Where the sunny day met the boundary of the storm there was a stunning alchemical fog of a furious wind blasting and conjoining sand, ocean spray and rain with sunlight turned diffuse and orange in a chaos of sensation.

Hawaiian legend holds that it is in this region that the spirits of the dead make their departure for the next world. The cocoon of orange light with rain and sand pellets assaulted me and launched me into a clearly altered state. In addition to the striking visual field, the acoustics seemed to form a murmuring drone that resembled human voices chanting a repetitive refrain, perfect for an excursion beyond the ordinary.

But the storm had created some very ordinary hazards on the road back. Many water-filled potholes were large enough to deserve names on a map and require fishing permits. There was no way to judge how deep they were, nor could we avoid all of them. We lurched and bounced ahead, coming upon a car whose radiator was well below sea level. Two young men stood helplessly beside it.

"You need some help there?," asked Joshua.

"Yeah, the axle is broke. Can you give us a lift?"

"Sure. Come on up."

The cab being full of us verging-on-carsick mainlanders, they boarded the truck bed and we lurched along, praying that we had not taken on our new passengers' vehicle karma. Near the cutoff to the main highway we passed a sodden cultivated field in which a large piece of farm machinery was poised at an awkward tilt and a young woman was going about her work. The fellows in the back of the truck hailed her.

"Yeah, we stick our car back there in the pothole. Broke the axle. Don't know what we gonna do."

"Yeah," she said, "I know some that stick theirs and earlier we stick this one" (pointing to the farm machine).

They carried on awhile about the hardships caused by the storm. Catching pieces of their conversation, I was reflecting on how we would have dealt with "sticking" our truck: walk until we had cell connection, arrange for a tow truck, and do what one does to get back to normal. What for us would be an inconvenience, to these individuals could easily be a profound hardship. In their shoes, would I have mentally amplified this inconvenience into a full-blown hardship? Had I become so soft and attached to agendas that this would rise to the level of emergency in my mind? Which was the problem—the situation itself or my appraisal of it? My attention was drawn back to the conversation that had by now established the fact that the situation sucked all around. The young woman paused thoughtfully, then looked up at the sky and swung her arm with hand upraised in a wide ark and announced for all to hear "But . . . It's a *beautiful* day!!!" We burst into laughter and headed on down the road.

I remembered calling Joshua and Annaleah, when they lost their 23 year old daughter last year. Mary—what a beautiful spirit—had struggled with the complications of a congenital heart defect and finally made her transition. Joshua's voice was breaking in a grief still powerful as the island storm. After awhile, he paused. "But . . . it's a beautiful day on Kaua'i." It was not with the exuberance of the young woman in the field, but it was nonetheless an affirmation of the spirit that soars above adversity and even death to touch the larger story.

How We Stick Ourselves

There are no limits to our ability to get stuck, to "stick" ourselves in the lesser story. Two factors conspire to keep us stuck. First is the Subconscious Mind, which warehouses imprints of all that we have experienced and have not made peace with. When cleansed of this debris, however, the subconscious is also a region of mind that can resonate with Divine Inspiration. Second is the universal human propensity to project blame—to see a person or thing "out there" as the source of our suffering. When these two are combined, you get war—between the sexes, between friends, colleagues, states, nations, or religions.

If I define something as a problem, whether it is a broken axle or a remark you made, something associated with it hooks onto it from the subconscious mind. Because subconscious content is beyond reach, we only are aware of the emotional charge. The here and now situation that is defined as a problem has become a much bigger problem than if the warehouse had been empty. If it's a remark you made, the emotional charge around every similar remark that I have not made peace with wells up. Because this internal arousal is so unpleasant, I project blame onto you to take my attention off my intolerable feelings.

This is a truly delusional state of mind that can take a problem that can be solved systematically with a minimum of bother and turn it into a nightmare. Or even if it cannot be solved presently, it can at least be viewed as difficult, but not catastrophic.

Our failure to deal with the subconscious and our tendency to blame others adds up to an inability to take responsibility for our lives. The feeling of powerlessness—and eventually hopelessness—that this engenders is an emotional cancer. If the Center for Disease Control dealt with emotional plagues, this stressful state of mind would be judged a pandemic. But this delusional state of mind is shared by nearly everyone, so it is regarded as normal.

There are many philosophies and techniques that have been developed, some recent and some ancient, for reducing stress. They all offer tools to help us move from helplessness to mastery of taking responsibility for ourselves. I can't take responsibility for the offensive remark you made to me, but I can, if I know how, take responsibility for my reaction to it—by cleaning the subconscious mind of all the experiences riding in on the coattails of the present situation. That greatly reduces the level of unpleasant arousal, so I don't have to project blame on you. Then I can comment on your remark without having to hit you with the full power of my emotion that flows from a history you had nothing to do with.

How We Get Unstuck

The ability to shift from a constricted state of awareness of insurmountable problems to a more transcendent view with a larger context depends on how much the subconscious is dominated by material from the past. But here the Hawaiian practice of Hoʻoponopono parts company with conventional problem-solving strategies. Hoʻoponopono, with ancient roots in Polynesia, means, roughly, "to make right." As traditionally conceived, it is a sophisticated method for interpersonal conflict resolution. However, noted Hawaiian healer Morrnah Nalamaku Simeona (1913-1992) adapted Hoʻoponopono to an *intra*personal context, fashioning a protocol that empowers an individual to work directly on the subconscious. But not only does this re-visioned Hoʻoponopono process reduce stress by erasing subconscious material, it also enlivens an ability of the subconscious to access the Superconscious Mind, the spiritual part of our makeup that is at one with Divinity.[1]

This clearer connection to Superconscious Mind allows Divine Inspiration to permeate all layers of mind and occupy the space vacated in the subconscious as a result of the erasing. True emotional freedom, in other words, consists not only of clearing up subconscious material, the true causes of our reactivity, but of the migration of Divine Inspiration into the territory once occupied by subconscious material.

It is this dual process of cleaning and invoking Inspiration that gives the freedom and flexibility to move from ʻīnea (suffering) to maluhia (peace). If we are caught in the clutches of the subconscious mind,

---

[1] Conventional psychology is unfortunately limited by its inability to acknowledge capacities beyond individual psychological structures.

saying "it's a beautiful day" is like wallpapering over lumpy plaster. You cannot fake it 'til you make it. Yet, when the right channels are open, you do not have to fake it. We are endowed with the capacity to experience peace. We only need to awaken to it.

In my mind I return often to Polihale. The confluence of wind, spray, driving sand and sun conspired in that strange storm to open a pathway to a clear place of refuge in my inner life in which I am capable of declaring "it's a beautiful day" even when I have stuck myself in a pothole. Kauaʻi gifted me with a story to illustrate a state of being that greets adversity as an opportunity to become aware of the light that it seems to be hiding.

Human beings do not like to change boats in midstream, especially streams of consciousness they had previously perceived as stable and declared holy

John Jay Harper

CHAPTER THREE

I Wouldn't Believe It, Even if it Were True

Don't ask me nothin' about nothin'.
I just might tell you the truth.

Outlaw Blues
Bob Dylan

To venture into the mindset of Hoʻoponopono requires a willingness to shift into what may be an unfamiliar frame of reference, for the process can pose a challenge when viewed from a rational perspective. Yet people's initial response is often a resounding "YES!," for only when the mind goes to work trying to understand the process intellectually do objections arise.

There is an immediate affirmation followed by doubt because there is a level of knowing that is more fundamental than the intellectual. We in the West are at a moment of shifting consciousness that permits us to connect with levels of truth that the rational mind can scarcely penetrate. This shift is undoing the inherited mindset, four hundred years in the making, that elevates the intellect to the position of gold standard. Thus, a reflexive tension can cause us to back away even from a very strong first impression of the rightness of an idea or practice.

Though the Ho'oponopono process does not require that we understand the changing perspectives, I nevertheless want to describe the intellectual bridge for readers to understand the dynamics of change as I did.

One of the things I have learned from practicing the Ho'oponopono process is that the understanding afforded by intellectual exercises is often more entertaining than it is transformational. And perhaps it is a way for a Western mind to get comfortable with the low dive before risking the high dive. In fact, a lesson gradually learned from the practice is that much of the thinking we do is counterproductive and serves to "stick" us. Ironically it is a bigger problem than it is purporting to solve. Since reservations are themselves due to subconscious factors, the Ho'oponopono process itself can obviate the need for understanding of the mind.

Dr. Larry Dossey, reviewing the literature on the effects of prayer on healing, found results based upon well-designed studies that were solidly convincing—including the efficacy of prayer at a distance. He quoted one scientist's reaction: "This is the sort of thing I would not believe, even if it really existed." The man was honest in acknowledging that even if the evidence were empirically sound, if it contradicted his rationalist paradigm, it had to be dismissed.

My own curiosity functioned like a "shoe horn" to ease me into a new way of thinking that is now a good fit. The western intellectual tradition validates perceptions by whether they stand up to the test of reason. Even if empirical validation can be supplied, if a given approach fails the test of reason, the results are often not taken seriously.

Nothing falls harder than a worldview. A worldview, in intellectual matters, sanctions a body of methodology—and even defines what is and what is not legitimate to study. Evidence that contradicts the established worldview is dismissed. Those who submit the evidence or use non-sanctioned methods are forced to recant or worse. Thomas Kuhn, a physicist and philosopher of science, in *The History of Scientific Revolutions*, described how knowledge progresses through time. It is a commonly held presumption that through human history, knowledge began as primitive perceptions and beliefs colored by superstition, then over millennia evolved gradually into the more accurate, more refined, rational, scientific worldview that we employ today. Kuhn's research, however, has established that this serial, linear, evolutionary model is mistaken. The growth of knowledge in fact is driven more by revolution than by evolution.

For a long time, discoveries outside the cultural paradigm are outrightly condemned. In modern times, UFO reports are explained as swamp gas, and crop circles as neighborhood pranks. These exemplify the tendency of the guardians of the existing paradigm to maintain their explanatory authority despite extensive evidence to the contrary. In an earlier era, Galileo was forced to recant his view that the sun, not the earth, is the center of the universe. Because the implications of this discovery contradicted the cosmological paradigm enforced by the Roman Catholic Church, he spent the rest of his life under house arrest.

As the human mind interacts with its world, observations, interpretations, and understandings coalesce into a paradigm—an overarching intellectual structure that gives definition to reality itself. Some accounts vary, but the arrival of English explorer Captain James Cook in 1779 was, for the residents of the island of Hawai'i, a profound spiritual event coinciding with the Makahiki, a celebration devoted to Lono, one of the major deities in the Hawaiian pantheon. Events cast him as a visitation of the god or his representative. This example illustrates how paradigms define what we perceive as real and how we interpret what we observe.

At that moment the prevailing Hawaiian paradigm was, in any case, about to undergo a radical transformation under the European agenda.

While investigators today need not fear for their lives, it is not unreasonable for them to fear for their livelihoods. Biophysicist Karl Popp, now widely recognized for his pioneering work on biophotons, for a substantial part of his career found himself out of work because the universities did not regard his work as real science. Today it is very difficult to find funding for any sort of scientific or intellectual work that strays very far from conventional perceptions of reality.

Paradigms begin to fall when investigators who are playing by the rules, peering ever more deeply into sanctioned subjects, employing approved methods, begin to discover with increasing frequency phenomena so exotic that they can simply no longer be explained away by accepted means. Then once the stalwart proponents of the old paradigm have died off, the world can be viewed afresh. New ideas and new methods, or very old ones that were previously considered taboo for serious investigation come out of the closet for consideration.

The relevance of this progression for Ho'oponopono is that we are now clearly in such a period of what Kuhn calls *abnormal science*. The passing standard has been referred to as the Newtonian/Cartesian paradigm after the two thinkers whose work most influenced the emerging worldview since the 17th century.

Many consider Sir Isaac Newton to be the greatest scientist of all time. His contributions revolutionized the mathematics and physics of his time. He is best known for his theories of motion and gravitation, an elegant conceptualization of the concrete principles by which objects in the universe interact with each other—described with a refined mathematics that he also fashioned.

French philosopher René Descartes is most recognized for his dictum *cogito ergo sum* (I think, therefore I am). In offering this formula, Descartes was attempting to arrive at knowledge that is certain beyond any doubt. The only thing I can know with absolute certainty is that thoughts arise—and because they arise to me, the "I" must exist. Furthermore, the soul in which these thoughts arise is essentially different from the body. While the body is a complex machine operating according to the laws of physics, with definite boundaries and location, the soul has no such physically definable properties. Therefore, it is non-material and is not controlled by the laws of physics. Soul and body—and by extension, soul and physical world—are completely separate, incommensurate domains. The term *Cartesian dualism* is used to describe this state of separation within the human being.

It is doubtful that either Newton or Descartes had any intention of shifting to a new paradigm. They were performing the work of physics, mathematics and philosophy, following their curiosities as they were led, drawing conclusions as best they knew how—within a cultural context. That they were simultaneously forming and being formed by their work was the foundation of the Age of Enlightenment, and while today we may doubt the accuracy of that term, it brought revolutionary shifts in the intellectual sphere—with a new paradigm defining the structure of reality and appropriate methods for arriving at clearer perceptions of reality.

The overarching conceptual contribution of Newton was that the entire universe is comprised of separate and distinct objects in empty space, which interact with each other according to mathematically definable laws—the universe as a gigantic machine. Even though it was too large for testing this hypothesis, the belief was that it functioned according to the same principles regardless of location or scale.

Descartes' irreconcilable split between mind and body, or soul and world, reinforced this theme of separateness. His logic that animals have no souls and his interests in the science of anatomy included dissection of live animals, for beings without souls can have no feelings. The further separation between human beings and the rest of creation gave grounds for exploitation of the natural world.

The ability to describe the physical world in such a compelling fashion began to erode the authority of institutional religion as the last word on the nature of reality. Even though the earliest formations of the Newtonian/Cartesian paradigm occurred after the Protestant Reformation, churches retained primary stewardship over the sacred domain. Although the newly emerging class of scientists was not subject to persecution by state religion, the splitting, separating dynamic of the new paradigm partitioned the relationship between science and religion into two distinct realms.

The loss of communication between these primary spheres of human activity came at great cost. Whereas the religious community via the Reformation had gained some relief from corrupt authority, this development can largely be viewed as a "freedom *from*." For the scientific community, on the other hand, the whole world lay ahead to be discovered. This "freedom *to*" opened a window on life that must have appeared brimming with promise and excitement. These new concepts, new discoveries, new methodologies stood in contrast to reformed religious practices that offered little new but the relief from old strictures. The *mana* clearly flowed toward and favored the exploration, description, and manipulation of the material world—and this condition came to define the western worldview. The split between soul and world proceeded into a devaluation of the domains of soul or mind. This led to conceiving mind as merely an epiphenomenon of biological material processes. This is nowhere more clearly exemplified today than in the treatment of mental disorders as *nothing but* biochemical imbalances.

While the Newtonian/Cartesian paradigm has made possible stupendous developments in science, technology and medicine, it has also created casualties. By splitting mind and body, it has alienated us from ourselves. By declaring material reality as the only domain worthy of being called real, it has alienated us from spiritual sources of emotional nurturance and meaning. By positing the human observer as unrelated to what is observed, it has alienated us from the natural world. The Newtonian/Cartesian paradigm gave the West the most sophisticated level of control over the environment, yet left us psychologically and spiritually empty.

The Newtonian/Cartesian paradigm received its first serious challenges from its own ranks in the early twentieth century, from the nascent discipline of quantum physics. The Newtonian view held up quite well, so long as we supposed that the minutest assemblages of matter consisted only of the tiniest of particles in motion according to the laws of motion. The atom depicted as a solar system in miniature illustrates this contention. However, as the early quantum physicists peered deeply into this level of existence, what they found was that matter—rather than being substantial or solid in any way—exists fundamentally as a *probability wave*. The act of observation forces the probability wave into a defined state that is then recognizable as matter.

What we call reality, then, is dependent upon the *consciousness* of an observer. By implication, there is no "out there" as a concretized material world. The perception of an "out there" is the result of the interaction of consciousness with a probability matrix. Thus, we are intimately involved in the creation of the world by sequential acts of perception, on a moment to moment basis.

Not only does the tree falling in the forest make no sound if there is no one to hear it, but there is neither tree nor forest. It gets stranger. "Particles" once in contact with each other continue to influence each other at a distance. Any distance. The behavior of one in Kansas City will be reflected in the other that may have moved to the other side of the galaxy. The effect, called *quantum entanglement* (Einstein, not wanting to believe it, called it "spooky action at a distance") is instantaneous—independent of any recognizable transmission of information. It is difficult to grasp the idea that we are implicated in the creation of the universe, and that the substrate of the material world is interconnected and integrated without regard to distance or time.

Consciousness as central to the structuring of reality, rather than merely observing, recording, or considering it—or, interconnection and interdependence, rather than separateness—defines the movement toward a new paradigm that is decisively different from the Newtonian/Cartesian view. It is interesting to note that the major figures in the development of the new science explored Eastern philosophy/mysticism and ancient Western philosophical writings in their attempts to find a vantage from which to understand these exotic discoveries, producing works such as *The Tao of Physics* by physicist Fritjof Capra. That spiritual studies formed a part of the background of scientific enterprise points to the possibility of a collaborative alliance of science with non-institutional spirituality—bridging yet another separation between these two domains.

A further development in new paradigm thinking is the discovery of the Zero Point Field. Whereas space was previously thought to be empty, it is now seen as an all-pervasive field from which all subatomic "particles" emerge and to which they return, in a ceaseless dynamic flux. The field as a unifying matrix stretches across the cosmos and through all levels and orders of magnitude of creation. While extraordinarily complex, the basic idea is that all the phenomena observed at a quantum level point to a unified field which is foundational and pervasive—the ultimate organizing and stabilizing factor in the universe. What appears to be empty space, whether between planets, stars, and galaxies—or between subatomic particles—is in fact, a pregnant void.

Some physicists of the new paradigm despair at the appropriation of their findings by the social sciences. Their concern, they explain, is with the most infinitesimal reaches of the material world—with little or no generalizability to such complex domains as human behavior or the behavior of whole systems. This parochial view is itself strangely old-paradigm in its insistence that the discoveries in one branch of knowledge should be segregated from the rest of human experience.

Consciousness, as the very medium of experience itself, is simultaneously the foundation from which the new paradigm of physics emerges, and the means by which the rest of the world comprehends it. Carl Jung introduced the notion of a collective unconscious or collective psyche as the dynamic, evolving substrate of personal and cultural awareness. In this instance it gives rise to both a new physical science and a new psychological science which both reflect a singular evolutionary movement within the collective psyche. These also invite the growth of consciousness itself to a new level, and may well integrate previously sequestered fields of human activity.

This growth, then, has the capacity to reach back into human history and prehistory to re-acquire and integrate the understandings of primal people whose practices and worldviews have generally been discarded by interim paradigms. Seemingly modern practices turn out to be reinventions of very old wheels. Shamans engaged in the most ancient healing practices used mental visualization exercises, much as do modern psychological and medical practice. At the same time, discovery of forgotten knowledge is accompanied by a fresh openness to ancient modalities practiced in their aboriginal ways. The proliferation of various tribal forms of the Native American sweat lodge ceremony exemplifies a growing respect for indigenous understandings and method—left to stand on their own, without "improvement." A third type of practice is a revision of an ancient method given by someone whose roots are in the culture in which the original practice evolved, such as Morrnah Simeona's internalized Ho'oponopono process.

The primary point is worth repeating—that the new paradigm in science places consciousness at the center of any discussion about the nature of reality. When the new paradigm is acknowledged as a product of an evolving collective consciousness, then all spheres of human endeavor will reflect the shift. Physics, as pure science, led the development this time—precisely because the recent paradigm had assigned to physical science the last word. But neither physics, nor science in general, can claim ownership of the understanding of reality that they spearheaded. The liberation from a perception that casts the world as a collection of separate objects—where matter is the only reality, and where consciousness is a by-product of neurochemistry—to a perception that consciousness is the agency that assembles reality, including matter and neurochemicals—is astounding. It is more astounding than the discovery that the earth circles the sun, rather than vice versa. It is so astounding, that for the most part, we have yet to awaken to how astounding it is, as well as to the liberation itself.

Our civilization has been plagued throughout its history because we have used old paradigm mastery over the world of matter without a parallel mastery of the capacities of the spirit. We have cultivated physics, engineering and economics while giving little attention to such faculties as wisdom, compassion and ecological ethics. The elevation of consciousness to its rightful place as the architect of reality invites us to ponder what values do we want our creation to reflect and promote.

In reality, however, we do not have to figure it out. Rather, we need to let go of the need to figure it out.

O ke ola no ʻia o kia ʻi loko

Look for the life within

CHAPTER FOUR

The Structure of Mind
or
Who Am I?

There is nothing "outside" to God
God is at the center and the
circumference of the cosmos at once—omnipresent.
God is in constant contact with every atom
and all life forms via the zero point field . . .

John Jay Harper
Tranceformers

The medical and spiritual practitioners of ancient Hawai'i developed a model of the psychospiritual structure of the human being that is as sophisticated as any that has been put forth in modern times. After the European contact, the history of Hawai'i has been that of a culture being dismantled. First by disease, then by missionaries, and then by big business, Hawaiians became divested of their identity in a way distressingly similar to the destruction of Amerindian civilization. Our kahuna friend, in telling stories of his childhood once explained that he was forbidden to speak his own language and was forced to study European history with no attention to his own. Hawaiian kupuna (elders) have been reluctant for a long time to reveal at any depth their understanding of the psychospiritual makeup of humans, having witnessed sacred knowledge too many times misused.

The Modern Western View of Mind

In the Hawaiian view, mind is a three-part structure. It bears some passing similarity to the Freudian model, which identifies the Ego, the organizing center of the Conscious Mind, and the Id, an unconscious reservoir of impulses and other psychic contents that are unacceptable to the Ego and held at bay by defense mechanisms. The partition of the psyche into conscious and subconscious spheres begins as the young child learns that certain behaviors and impulses are unacceptable to the parents. The Superego consists of an internalization of those parental proscriptions—a sort of psychic *in loco parentis*—and also the ego ideal—the moral/ethical aspiration which guides behavior. The goal of Freudian psychoanalysis is to guide the unconscious into awareness, thereby expanding the sphere of influence of the Ego and allowing a greater degree of self-acceptance and self-mastery. This model leaves the Ego in a more or less perpetual state of conflict between the demands of the unconscious Id for total expression and gratification, and the Superego, which exerts the force of moral restraint.

Jung concurred that there was a psychic storehouse of repressed material and instinctual pressures—which he renamed the personal unconscious. And he identified a deeper level of the unconscious—the collective unconscious, a field of experience common to all humankind and therefore a foundation upon which individual existence is erected. This field is organized into archetypes, fundamental patterns of psychic life that most often manifest on an individual level in dreams and on a collective level in mythology.

It is at the level of the collective unconscious that the spiritual life is engendered. Jung referred to the central organizing archetype as the Self—often represented and experienced as a God image in the psyche. He maintained that psychology could neither prove nor disprove the existence of God, it can only assert with certainty that there is a *God image* at the dynamic center of the personality. Over his door, however, was the inscription "Bidden or unbidden God is here."

A collective unconscious implies that there is a field of awareness not limited to a particular person, an awareness that is transpersonal. Yet, the collective unconscious is an aspect of an individual person's makeup, allowing a person to be a discreet entity and also identify with the totality of all that exists. At a different level of discourse this is the same dilemma concerning how to regard a subatomic quantum as both a particle and a wave. There is no way to resolve this paradox intellectually, for it depends on your momentary vantage point, since both observations are true.

Jung's perspective was highly controversial. It found few friends in the Freudian community, and was the key element in the break between Freud and Jung. It similarly found no home in the halls of academic psychology. These cloistered spheres were the embodiments of the Newtonian/Cartesian paradigm expressing in the psychological sciences. The notion of an aspect of mind that is universal or *transpersonal* was generally regarded as a religious or mystical notion that had no place in scientific discourse. But the shift in consciousness activated by the quantum revolution and reflected in Jung's formulation was simply too strong to be silenced by official censure. The field of Transpersonal Psychology emerged as the representative of the quantum revolution in psychology, and as a discipline open to the contributions of all fields of knowledge and experience—ancient and modern, Eastern and Western.

Based upon now fifty years of consciousness research, Transpersonal Psychology has been able to assert that in an ordinary state the human mind perceives itself to be a discrete entity, separate from other minds, yet in alternate states it recognizes itself as potentially commensurate with all creation—we are no longer, as Alan Watts says, "skin-encapsulated egos."

Many of us have had moments in life that Maslow termed peak experiences. Usually they are experienced as deeply peaceful and/or joyful, feeling expansive or profound connectedness—as if we and our surroundings are one. Different traditions have maintained that this transcendent state is present and available to us at all times. It is not so much a matter of creating it as of removing the obstacles to realizing it—like on a cloudy day, with the sun still present. We may be living in subdued light, but this is not because the source of light is diminished. In a very real sense, we are always in this condition of *the one mind*, although we are generally consciously identified only with that parcel of it associated with our name. The Ego identity is discrete in time and space and takes conscious awareness as its platform of operations. The Self Identity is the totality of creation itself.

Intellect is the default faculty Ego has to make sense of the world, and the world that the intellect digests as its raw data is therefore circumscribed by the boundaries of conscious Ego. The best the intellect can do is point to the broader and deeper realities from which it is thus constrained. For a person totally identified with the Ego and its intellect, transpersonal realities seem fraudulent, mere productions of fantasy. For one whose accounts with reality are not so altogether closed, the larger presence may bleed through enough to convey an intuition of a larger reality.

Direct experience is the avenue that removes all doubt. When one experiences a heightened state of awareness of the world, the intellect settles into a role subordinate to the expanded reality. A good example of this phenomenon is what has become called the near death experience

(NDE). Numerous books have been written about this by experiencers as well as by researchers in medicine and psychology. People who die in accidents and in operating rooms but are resuscitated after several minutes frequently report having left their bodies to travel through tunnels toward a being of light, then reuniting with loved ones and entering a world of expansive beauty. Usually the experience is reported as vividly real, more real than ordinary waking life. This report is consistent with those of visionaries and shamans who also value a higher reality to this non-ordinary state than to ordinary reality. They are not persuaded by the attempts of non-experiencers to explain the phenomena as a function of degraded biochemical processes in the brain at the threshold of death.

The practical operation of Ho'oponopono does not depend upon entering such non-ordinary states of awareness, yet the map of the psyche by which it may be understood is very much in keeping with the understanding of life that such states reveal. Ho'oponopono allows the practitioner to be fully present in this world of everyday life, while having a connection to the larger reality from which energy can flow into the compressed reality of mundane life.

The Hawaiian View of the Structure of Mind

The Hawaiians had long ago evolved an understanding of the mind from the transpersonal perspective. The three Hawaiian terms used to describe the structural elements of the mind originate in the exoteric spiritual world view of Hawai'i, particularly of the pre-Christian era: 'uhane—the spirit or soul, 'unihipili—the spirit of a deceased person, and 'aumakua—a family or personal god or ancestral spirit.

The notion of the 'unihipili as the spirit of a deceased person is interesting in its application to inner psychological states. In dreams, material that has been repressed from conscious waking awareness can be symbolized by the unconscious mind as a corpse. It is not dead literally, but it has been buried and lies in the unconscious in a frozen, unchanging, inactive, unresponsive state. When we find ourselves stuck in a pattern of thinking, feeling, behaving and relating that repeatedly causes us suffering, we are experiencing one of these subconscious "dead" parts of ourselves doing its zombie walk.

'Uhane, as the spirit or soul, is more of the nature of the existence and self-awareness of a person who is alive, growing, making choices, and functioning in life as an independent entity. It is the essence that we identify as "my" indwelling spirit or soul that makes it possible for us to be conscious and aware of our own existence separate from, but in relation to, other beings.

'Aumakua, as family or personal god or ancestral spirit, is the link between my spirit as 'uhane, and the larger realm of spiritual beings. These beings are of a higher order of perceptiveness, knowledge, wisdom and power, and can also serve as the intermediaries between an individual and higher spiritual realms. The notion of the po'e 'aumākua indicates that the domain of 'aumākua is interwoven and interconnected, that the wholeness or oneness of all life and consciousness is a given. [2]

When the Hawaiians translated this hierarchy of the spiritual realm into an internal classification of the levels of mind is difficult to determine. Yet it is characteristic of most spiritual systems to carry an inner, esoteric, more profound understanding that outlines a pathway to fundamental truth than can be found in the exoteric, common practices. Esoteric practices include Qabbala in Judaism, Sufism in Islam and the monastic traditions in Buddhism and Christianity—the mystical branches of the respective faiths. These branches support individuals who seek to move beyond ecclesiastical practices into an exploration and direct experience of creation itself, using Self as vehicle. The concept that to know this Self is to know the All is common to all varieties of mysticism.

---

[2]   'aumakua=singular, 'aumākua=plural

Consistent with this principle, the *internal* Hawaiian cosmos uses the designations *'Uhane*, *'Unihipili* and *'Aumakua* to delineate a dynamic hierarchy of psychospiritual structure. Typically the terms are capitalized when used in this fashion to distinguish them from the traditional usage. In this characterization, 'Uhane corresponds to Conscious Mind or Middle Self, 'Unihipili to Subconscious Mind or Low Self, and 'Aumakua to Superconscious Mind or High Self. Although this rendering is open to debate, the esoteric meanings comprise the structural model of the mind put forth by a number of writers and practitioners, including Morrnah Simeona.

A fourth level—Divinity—is in one sense above the other three, yet is at the same time inherent within the three. As both transcendent and immanent it is the critical element in this system. This structure is graphically represented in Figure 1[3].

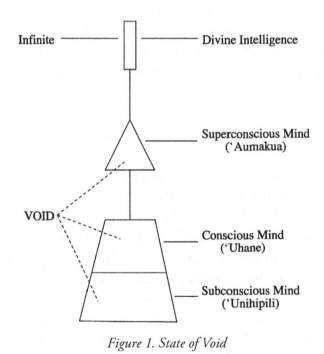

Figure 1. State of Void

---

[3]   All figures reproduced by permission from IZI LLC.

This schematic representation of the mind expresses its fundamental structure—its pristine state before any difficult life experience has left its mark—and its nature as a perfect expression of Divine Intelligence, which is pure, undifferentiated potential. When this primal, foundational status of mind is active, it is called being "in the zero state" or "at zero." This is the psychospiritual equivalent of the "pregnant void" or "zero point field" of physics, as well the void or empty states cultivated in mystical practices. It is not a void or zero that implies an absolute absence. Rather, it is a state of absolute, undifferentiated and dynamic potential.

This condition speaks to a truth so simple that it risks escaping notice— the unadorned answer to the question "Who am I?" The entire purpose of the Hoʻoponopono process is to restore us to who we are, a three-part self, fully containing and expressing the Divine. This unity of the three-part self with the Divine is called Self I-dentity—the "I" referring to the Divine as in-forming our true nature through the structures of mind. The purpose of our lives is to remove the obstructions to the "I" becoming fully resident throughout triune mind.

In its pristine, uncorrupted, original state, Self I-dentity is suffused with and characterized by Divine Intelligence. "I and my Father" are One. My will is one with the Divine will. I am in the flow, in the Tao. This paradox is commonly found in mystical traditions—that the fullness of individual identity occurs in the letting go of any claim to an ultimately separate, circumscribed self.

It was always puzzling to me that those teachers and elders who lay great emphasis on the insubstantiality and even illusion of self, seem to display the best-developed and healthiest sense of self I had seen. How paradoxical that the pinnacle of unique individuality as a personality is achieved while simultaneously yielding all pretensions thereto. As we walk these paths, paradox arises frequently and is experienced as a delight rather than as a problem.

The 'Unihipili, though at the bottom, is perhaps the most complex structure in this characterization. Thought of as a "body mind" it is responsible for the operation of the extraordinarily complex and intricate self-regulatory processes of physical existence—respiration, digestion, immune function, circadian rhythms, and so forth. As Subconscious Mind, it is also the archive of memory data—both personal and transpersonal—that gives rise to our experience of problems in living. As the source of habitual behavior, it is partial to routine and highly subject to conditioning. As the intermediary between 'Uhane and 'Aumakua it is the means by which our conscious wishes and intentions are conveyed to Divinity.

It is 'Uhane that has the capacity to choose, which is essential in the Ho'oponopono process, for without choice, there is no process.

'Aumakua is the spiritual essence of the individual, that aspect of mind that is always in communion with the spiritual Source. It lives in Eternal time and contains the map of our destiny and the knowledge of how we interface with the totality of existence.

The Hawaiian View of the Energetics of Mind

In addition to the three structural elements and Divinity, there are dynamic energy pathways among the structures. The internal flow of mana from 'Uhane is unidirectional. Its trajectory is toward 'Unihipili. The flow of mana from 'Unihipili is bi-directional. It can send mana toward 'Uhane in the form of memories replaying—which is experienced by 'Uhane (me) as any of a host of problem states. It can also send mana directly to 'Aumakua, bypassing 'Uhane, in the form of prayers, wishes, desires, or petitions that are initiated by 'Uhane. The flow of mana from 'Aumakua is also bi-directional. It can send mana to the Divine in the form of requests it has received from 'Unihipili, refined from its higher perspective, and mana from the Divine can be transmitted by 'Aumakua to ʻUhane and then to ʻUnihipili to bring about cleansing and healing in all the structures.

While this description may seem theoretical now, it will make sense when we begin to discuss the dynamics of *cleaning*, the central process in Hoʻoponopono practice. What is useful to note is that any petition to the Divine, whether consciously conceived or not, passes first through ʻUnihipili. The petition must go down before it can go up. This description expresses a truth known to transpersonal psychologists that the Subconscious Mind must be addressed in any comprehensive understanding of spirituality, for it has the power to either assist or impede our practices. The lower mind is truly the doorway to the higher mind.

How We Forget Who We Are

We are a threefold self that embraces and is embraced by a fourth— Divinity or God. The process of Hoʻoponopono cleanses us of the obstacles that come between us and the realization of who we are. The obstacles may be the internalized aspects of experiences we were unable to cope with consciously that have accumulated over time. Additionally, the expanded model of the psyche presented by transpersonal psychology and ancient Hawaiian understandings includes the collective woes of the cosmos in the subconscious burden. Thus anything that presents itself as a problem to us is the reflection of a disturbance that is the same in me as in you—the same in anyone anywhere and anywhen in the cosmos.

The experience that manifests for me from this core phenomenon may be different from the experience for you. The core that is common to both is what is called a *memory* in Hoʻoponopono circles. What we usually think of as a memory is the recollection of a mental image or series of images that has thoughts and feelings attached to it. When Ho'oponopono practitioners refer to memory, it is not memory as recollection, but as a bit of information in the cosmos that does not take on a specific assemblage of image, thought and emotion until it is configured as an experience by the mind of an individual. The memory is a logjam in the flow of energy in the cosmos. I may experience the logjam as fear and frustration over a disturbance in my relationship with my boss. You may experience it as anger over a bolt twisting off as you're attempting to change a tire. The sun may experience it as a coronal disturbance set off by the current gravitational configuration of objects in the solar system.

While the first manifestations of the memory in my personal experience may be made conscious, the memory itself can never be made conscious. I might be able to trace the specific nature of the disturbance in my relationship with my boss as stemming from a traumatic experience I had with my father that has predisposed me to have certain stresses in my relationships with male authority figures. While this insight may help me separate what is past from what is present and thereby reduce the tension somewhat, it does not reach to the dynamic core of the issue. Insight cannot penetrate to the level of memory in this sense, only to the earliest manifestations of memory as they played themselves out in my experience.

Once the Subconscious Mind has become filled with memories, our experience of life is dominated by them and their patterns of interplay. Though we think we are free people making free choices, we do not know that we are being driven by patterns below the level of awareness. When the structures of mind are suffused with true freedom, the replaying of memories is replaced by the presence of the Divine, which is called Inspiration. These two states constitute the two tracks that our experience moves along, depending on what we are willing to do. These opposing configurations are represented in Figure 2.

The figure on the right shows the deluded state in which we, as conscious mind, believe ourselves to be free but are, in fact, under the sway of memories replaying in the subconscious. The left hand figure shows the state of inspiration, in which memories have been erased and the Divine has taken up residence in all strata of the mind.

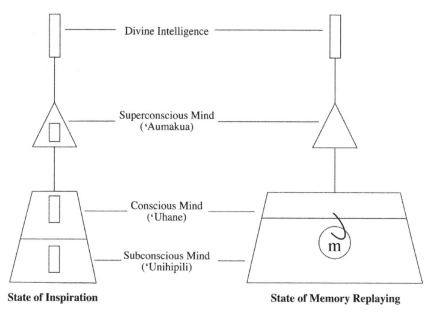

Figure 2. The structure of mind with Divine Inspiration established in all regions (represented by presence of ☐ in each level) vs. mind disturbed with memories replaying (where ☐ is outside the individual's access)

The state of memories replaying, unchallenged by any effective practice to recognize and transmute them, eventually paralyzes the Conscious Mind and traps it in a hopeless enterprise of trying to figure itself and the world out. Ironically, Conscious Mind seized in the throes of memories replaying, fancies itself to be in control. This delusion renders it further ineffectual in making sense of life and knowing how to relate to it. Cut off from useful ways of engaging both subconscious and superconscious resources, it is alone and impotent to understand the larger tasks of creating a life with meaning, purpose and value. This condition is evident in the prevalence of addiction, anxiety, depression and a host of other ills symptomatic of mind ignorant of its true nature and of the meaning of problems.

The description of the mind, the circuitry of mana, and the relation of these processes to Divinity set the stage for a vision of how healing happens, and how it happens simultaneously in the Self and in the world.

Self I-dentity is indestructible and eternal as its creator, Divine Intelligence. The consequence of ignorance is the false reality of senseless and relentless poverty, disease and war and death generation after generation.

'Ihaleakalā Hew Len, Ph.D.

CHAPTER FIVE

Picking Up Stones

Each child born has at birth, a Bowl of perfect Light. If he tends his Light it will grow in strength and he can do all things, swim with the shark, fly with the birds, know and understand all things. If, however, he becomes envious or jealous he drops a stone into his Bowl of Light and some of the Light goes out. Light and the stone cannot hold the same space. If he continues to put stones in the Bowl of Light, the Light will go out and he will become a stone. A stone does not grow, nor does it move. If at any time he tires of being a stone, all he needs to do is turn the bowl upside down and the stones will fall away and the Light will grow once more.

Pali Jae Lee
Ho'opono

This parable from Moloka'i illustrates the point that in its pristine state the structure of mind is suffused with and is a perfect expression of

Divinity. It implies that this structure undergoes a distortion when a person, for whatever reasons, takes on emotional burdens and moves out of the zero state.

When our Bowl of Light has stones in it, we are no longer free beings. The experiences that constitute the unfolding of our lives are less and less the reflection of our Divine nature and more and more the replaying of repetitious patterns generated by imprints residing in our Subconscious Mind.

Compared to the weightlessness of Light, stones are heavy. It is no surprise that the language of emotional suffering contains metaphors of heaviness: "he has a heavy burden to carry," "she's pulling a lot of baggage." The parable of the Bowl implies that the Light is a fundamental ground of our existence. It may be displaced or covered over by the psychological burdens we acquire, but these obscurations only have the power to cloud over, not to destroy. During a storm, the sun shines as brightly as on a clear day. The Divine is no less present in the subconscious of a mind full of memories replaying than in a clear mind—but it is clouded and less accessible.

From a psychoanalytic perspective, filling the bowl with stones is a product of conflict between the spontaneous expressions of impulse gratification and the negative consequences delivered by the parental environment, traumas, accidents, etc. All experience that a person cannot digest and assimilate is consigned to and imprinted in the subconscious. From the spiritual perspective, the subconscious is also the warehouse of misdeeds and deluded understanding and behavior that the soul has archived since the time of its creation. It may even go beyond the human level to include any disharmony in any system of the cosmos.

In place of the original, unadulterated state of being are the manifestations of imprints that are unconscious, static, unchanging, "stuck" spots that Ho'oponopono terms *memories*. The rocks in our Bowls of Light.

To turn the Bowl over, what is first required is tiring of being a stone. That is, when we tire of playing the same old script unendingly. Perhaps it comes in the midst of a third marriage—three spouses, same problems. Or a fifth friendship that ends in feeling abandoned or betrayed. Perhaps a major illness or mid-life crisis causes us to re-evaluate our whole outlook on life. It might be a profound welling up of sadness and compassion while reflecting upon the waves of suffering we witness on the news.

An interviewer once asked a psychologist "Doctor, is it true that life is one damned thing after another?" "No," the psychologist replied, "Life is the same damned thing over and over again." In *Simple Spirituality* I told the story of a client who discovered that he and his wife were having the same basic arguments over and over. He thought a great time and energy saver would be to number them and simply scream "NUMBER FOUR!"—rather than go through the whole routine. If we look closely at what worries us or what problems come up in daily life, there is usually nothing terribly novel. Unprecedented things do arise, but the bulk of our anguish is a repetition of perpetual issues—*memories replaying*. The underlying unchanging, static and heavy quality to our perennial complaints indeed feels like a collection of stones. The critical juncture in our journey arises when, to use a phrase from Alcoholics Anonymous, we are "sick and tired of being sick and tired."

After I wrote the preliminary lines of this chapter, Judith asked me to please come out and help her trim a large bush which had overgrown a part of our driveway. As I plowed into it, my clippers kept hitting a solid object. After I had cleared away a gaggle of small branches I was able to get enough leverage on the object to pull it out. It was a flower pot filled to the top with rocks! When one is in a state of flow, synchronicities of this sort become a delightful indication of the presence of the Divine in the midst of the mundane—which imbues the mundane with the sacred.

When we are at zero, we do not experience anything or anyone as a problem. The world is perfect the way it is presenting itself at this moment. When we are at zero, we feel no conflict or compulsion. If conditions require action, that action flows through us in a natural and matter of fact way. Perhaps language makes this process sound robotic. What if we have just witnessed an accident and we need to tend to the injured, call 911, and remove people from vehicles about to explode? Can you imagine that it is *possible* to do all these things quickly, efficiently and effectively without feeling frightened and agitated? Are terror and inner turmoil there to make us act more effectively? Or might our actions be effective *in spite of* this agitated inner state, which is, in fact, both unnecessary and interfering? I would guess most of us would tend to believe that this sort of agitated state of arousal spurs us into a quick response. It is an appropriate fight or flight reaction engineered by our neurological hardware. Yet it *is* possible to witness such an event from the zero state—and to remain in the zero state while responding to it with maximum effectiveness.

It is important to begin to understand this paradigm shift. Whenever we are confronted with a situation in life which we experience as a problem, a difficulty, or an emergency, what we are primarily experiencing first and foremost is a memory replaying in the subconscious zone of mind. The situation "out there" is not what hijacks our awareness and defines it as a problem. That is how we are conditioned to think of it, and we assume that that is just the way it is. The only thing we know is how our mind structures incoming information. When a bee flies into the room, the room revealed to the bee through its sensory and cognitive apparatus is very different world from that revealed to us. Which perception is correct?

Our tendency to see problems as coming to us from the outside is the result of a long process of cultural indoctrination. The flu bug, the tyrant boss, the difficult spouse, the interminable telephone voice menu (listen closely because our menu has changed!) all *make me* crazy. But the idea that my craziness is *their* fault is not just the cultural paradigm. Because my Subconscious Mind is not conscious, the whole process happens outside my awareness. Just as Copernicus discovered that the sun does not orbit the earth but vice versa, we need to be open to the idea that what seems obvious to us about the nature of our state of mind may be very different from the obvious.

Willingness to consider that what we experience as life is not what comes at us from outside but what we are unconsciously generating from inside—this is a huge revisioning of the nature of our lives. If we can allow that the Hawaiian theory of the structure of mind is plausible and potentially provides a map that leads out of the wilderness, and that the reality we experience is as this theory describes, we can proceed to a discussion of how to use this theory in a practical, problem solving, and life-liberating way.

Though this process did not originate with a Hawaiian psychologist, it was the reported experience of a Hawaiian psychologist practicing Ho'oponopono that accelerated its proliferation throughout the world as a modality for problem solving and liberation. The next chapter will focus on this individual and how he has offered the practice to the world.

Without going outside,
  you may know the whole world.
Without looking through the window,
  you may see the ways of heaven.

The farther you go, the less you know.

Thus the sage knows without traveling;
  He sees without looking;
  He works without doing.

Lao Tsu

CHAPTER SIX

The Rainmaker

A story from *Mysterium Coniunctionis* by C.G. Jung:

There was a great drought where [Richard] Wilhelm lived; for months there had not been a drop of rain and the situation became catastrophic. The Catholics made processions, the Protestants made prayers, and the Chinese burned joss-sticks and shot off guns to frighten away the demons of the drought, but with no result.

Finally the Chinese said, "We will fetch the rain-maker." And from another province a dried up old man appeared. The only thing he asked for was a quiet little house somewhere, and there he locked himself in for three days.

On the fourth day the clouds gathered and there was a great snow-storm at the time of the year when no snow was expected, an unusual amount, and the town was so full of rumors about the wonderful rain-maker that Wilhelm went to ask the man how he did it.

In true European fashion he said: "They call you the rain-maker; will you tell me how you made the snow?"

And the little Chinese said: "I did not make the snow; I am not responsible."

"But what have you done these three days?"

"Oh, I can explain that. I come from another country where things are in order. Here they are out of order; they are not as they should be by the ordinance of heaven. Therefore the whole country is not in Tao, and I also am not in the natural order of things because I am in a disordered country. So I had to wait three days until I was back in Tao and then naturally the rain came."

—p. 419-20 Mysterium Coniunctionis: an Inquiry into the Separation and Synthesis of Psychic Opposites in Alchemy, vol. 14 Bollingen Series XX: **The Collected Works of C. G. Jung**, 2d edition, trans by R.F.C. Hull, Princeton University Press 1976.

In another one of those profound paradoxes of spiritual practice, the rainmaker says "I am not responsible," when it appears that he has taken full responsibility by bringing himself into Tao when all is disordered around him. The only work of the rainmaker is to permit balance to come *within himself.* When one is in Tao, that is, in alignment with Divinity, the surrounding world comes into balance. The religious practitioners in the story were attempting to work on the outer conditions, to no avail.

It is interesting to note that snow rather than rain was the outcome. When major rain breaks a drought cycle, the parched ground cannot absorb the sudden influx, so the rain runs off as flash-flooding. The snow, melting slowly, softens the arid ground and permits a gradual absorption of the needed moisture. This is no small point. The rainmaker did not assume that he knew what was best. He did not pray for rain, speak to the rain spirits, or visualize rain. He allowed himself to return to the state of balance to which he was accustomed, and Divinity provided the specific—and absolutely correct—solution to the problem.

The Snow Fell Also on Oʻahu

I always uncheck the box that asks "may we send you information about updates" and check the one that, in effect, says "I don't wish to hear from anyone else you think I may want to hear from." So why do I keep getting all this junk mail? My wireless connection must have a direct link to someone's trash. My finger was on the delete button but the terms "Hawaiian," "psychologist" and "shaman" caught my eye. Whoever's trash bin this came from looked like one I could rummage around in for awhile. I read on about a Hawaiian psychologist who had worked on a hospital unit for the criminally insane. Apparently the unit was truly the nightmare such places are cracked up to be. I had never worked at a facility for the criminally insane, but earlier in my career had served as a staff psychologist on the locked inpatient psychiatric unit at a V.A. hospital. While every effort was made to give good care, these facilities seem inherently dark, depressing and, at times, frightening. Reportedly, there was major staff absenteeism and turnover, not surprising as staff was routinely threatened and assaulted. I could only imagine what a similar unit, but for the *criminally* insane, might be like.

This psychologist apparently had successfully treated patients on a high security unit for male patients who had committed violent criminal acts. The email went on to say that this psychologist never did any sort of psychotherapy or counseling with any of these patients. What he did

was go over patients' charts in his office, and as he did he engaged the Ho'oponopono process of repentance, forgiveness and transmutation for himself. As he continued to work on himself, the patients improved, as did the entire emotional atmosphere of the unit.

In *Zero Limits*, co-authored by the psychologist, 'Ihaleakalā Hew Len and Joe Vitale, the state hospital experience and the Ho'oponopono process are explored as a narrative of Vitale's journey into and immersion in the world of Ho'oponopono practice. Dr. Hew Len describes the hospital experience in detail.

It is true that:

1. I spent several years as a fee-paid service staff psychologist at Hawai'i State Hospital, psychiatric facility operated by the Hawai'i State Health Department.
2. I spent three years from 1984 to 1987 as the staff psychologist, 20 hours a week, in a high-security unit housing male patients who had committed criminal acts of murder, rape, drug use, and assault and battery against people and property.
3. When I entered the high-security unit in 1984 as the staff psychologist, all seclusion rooms were occupied with violent patients.
4. On any given day on the unit there were several patients in metal restraints around their ankles and wrists to prevent violence against others.
5. Violence on the unit by patients against patients and patients against staff was a common occurrence.
6. Patients were not intimately involved in their care and rehabilitation.
7. There were no in-unit rehabilitative work activities.
8. There were no off-unit activities, recreation, or work.
9. Visits by families on the unit were extremely rare.

10. No patients were allowed off the high-security unit without written permission by the psychiatrist and only with ankle and wrist restraints.
11. The stay in the unit by a typical patient ran into years, the cost being, I believe, around $30,000 a year then.
12. Staff sick leave ran extremely high on the ward.
13. The physical environment on the unit was drab and somewhat rundown.
14. The unit staff was composed of basically wonderful and caring people.
15. What I've described is probably typical of most psychiatric units elsewhere in the country.

When I left the unit and facility in July, 1987:

1. Seclusion rooms were no longer in use.
2. Wrist and ankle restraints were no longer in use.
3. Violent acts were extremely rare, usually involving new patients.
4. Patients were responsible for their own care, including arranging residential, work, and legal services before leaving the unit and the facility.
5. Off-unit recreational activities such as jogging and tennis were ongoing, not requiring approval by a psychiatrist or the use of ankle and wrist restraints.
6. Off-unit work activities were begun, such as car washing, without the approval of a psychiatrist or the use of ankle and wrist restraints.
7. Off-unit work consisted of baking cookies and polishing shoes.
8. Visits in the unit by family were taking place.
9. Staff sick leave was not a chronic problem.
10. The unit environment greatly improved with painting and maintenance and because people cared.

11. The unit staff was more involved in supporting patients to be 100 percent responsible for themselves.
12. The turnaround time for patients from admission to leaving the hospital was greatly reduced to months instead of years.
13. The quality of life for both patients and staff shifted dramatically from being custodial to one of family, people caring for one another.

What did I do for my part as the unit staff psychologist? I did the Self I-dentity through Ho'oponopono process of repentance, forgiveness, and transmutation for whatever was going on in me that I experienced consciously and unconsciously as problems before, during, and after leaving the unit each time.
I did not do any therapy or counseling with patients on the unit.
I did not attend any staff conferences on patients.
I took 100 percent responsibility for myself to clean with the stuff in me that caused me problems as staff psychologist.[4]

Dr. Hew Len's account and the changes that took place were corroborated in the book by hospital personnel serving at the same time.

Hearing of Dr. Hew Len's work resonated with me on a deep level. Though my western mind generated its expected critique, I found something inside me saying a resounding "YES" to what I was hearing. Perhaps it was in part due to the emphasis on working on oneself, that value seemingly lost on the new generation of psychotherapists. Here was a psychologist advocating how vital the inner work of the therapist is in the healing process. But, wow, he was taking that idea to a new level! Through an inner process of cleaning his own mind of whatever came up in response to his experience of the patients and staff, the world around him was transformed. This was consciousness altering the

---

4   Vitale, Joe and Hew Len, 'Ihaleakalā. (2007). *Zero Limits: The Secret Hawaiian System for Wealth, Health, Peace and More.* Hoboken, NJ: John Wiley & Sons, Inc., 140-142.

quantum environment—at a level where the distinction between inner and outer ceases to have meaning.

The implications of this understanding of the mind and its capabilities is profound. From the standpoint of psychotherapy, it is saying that a diagnosis and treatment plan are, at best, conventions of the way a therapeutic relationship is structured, and by how it must be represented in our culturally sanctioned healing and reimbursement rituals. Both the patient's presenting complaints and the therapist's evaluation and intervention are more than likely the products of memories replaying. Without direct reference to the quantum, zero state, little real healing is possible.

The assertion that the world receives healing when I effectively invite healing into myself suggests that I must take total responsibility for whatever my mind renders to conscious awareness as a problem. What Hoʻoponopono calls memories are distributed throughout the quantum field. Because my Self I-dentity is one with that field, if I somehow succeed in eliminating it, it is eliminated.

Where this may seem confusing is in the particular use of the term *memory.* What is meant is not, for example, a memory of how my father abused me, or how I felt abandoned when my brother was born, or any memory archived in my Subconscious Mind that could potentially be made conscious. Memory in the Hoʻoponopono sense is more like a seed of pure information, a data point that exists in the collective psyche and in the cosmos at large. It may have manifested in my own experience as an episode of abuse or abandonment plus all the thoughts and feelings that went with it. It is not the same as my recollections of my anxieties during my first day at school. While we refer to this as a memory in common parlance, Hoʻoponopono views these images, thoughts and feelings as products of, or representations of, the memory. The memory itself is a phenomenon of stuck, unmetabolized energy. A rock in the Bowl of Light.

Another way of understanding a memory is as a piece of raw data that has separated itself off from the energetic flow of experience. This data point may show up in consciousness on one occasion as a recollection of anxiety on the first day of school, on another as my anger at a motorist cutting me off in traffic while I was test driving a new car. The point is that the specific recollection, or even current problematic circumstance, is not what Hoʻoponopono terms a memory. While the manifestation can be known, the memory itself is unknowable, and does not need to be known for the process to work. We can explore the manifestation of memory forever through psychoanalytic uncovering and working-through, but until the memory has itself been erased, the experiences it serves up will simply move on to the next representation.

Taking 100% Responsibility

When I become aware of a situation you are involved in and experience it as a problem, because it is in my awareness I must take full responsibility for it. *My taking responsibility does not mean that I take on the blame for or burden of what happened to you.* It means that I accept the fact that the *underlying memory* is in the cosmos, and, therefore, also in me. It also means that I can clean it in me and thereby relieve both you and me of the component of suffering for which it is responsible. The decision to clean is a personal act that links to the transpersonal domain—and the method employed for the cleaning process is the energetic bridge between them. While the Conscious Mind that initiates the cleaning process is bounded, the cleaning method operates on an unbounded, transpersonal level.

The number of memories or bits of information that may aggregate to manifest as given experience can be considerable. This is why Dr. Hew Len cleaned for several years at Hawaiʻi State Hospital. Cleaning cannot be taken on half-heartedly—yet the commitment to practice it need not be burdensome. It is simply a matter of engaging the Conscious Mind to do something worthwhile in moments that we normally waste in rambling internal monologue and trying to figure things out.

Dr. Hew Len often refers to *The User Illusion* by Tor Norretranders, which cites research indicating that the conscious mind is capable of processing only 12-40 bits of information per second compared to hundreds of millions of bits per second flowing in the subconscious. The sheer quantity of subconscious material overtaxes the conscious mind when it takes the role of problem solver or issue resolver. It is simply not equipped for this process. While Conscious Mind can promote analysis and understanding of a problem, deep healing can only occur when the subconscious itself becomes the site of intervention—and because the subconscious domain is so vast, this requires a radical and far-reaching process.

Someday, after we have mastered the winds,
the waves, the tides and gravity,
we shall harness for God the energies of love.
And then, for the second time in the history of
the world, man will have discovered fire.

Pierre Teilhard de Chardin

CHAPTER SEVEN

Cleaning
Making Snow With Ho'oponopono

If "thank you" were the only prayer we ever said, it would be enough.

Meister Eckart

To understand what turning the bowl over means in the Ho'oponopono way, we must understand the process already referred to as *cleaning*. As it unfolds, the Light that has been present all along begins to shine through more and more, and we increasingly step into our Divine Self I-dentity. Rather than our life being confounded by memories replaying, we increasingly live in a state of Divine Inspiration.

Ka Pu'uhonua—The City of Refuge

In the times before contact with the western world, Hawai'i's social system included an institution called the *pu'uhonua*, a place or city of refuge. These were sacred places that were safe havens for those who needed protection for various reasons—women and children in times of war, individuals who had violated a law, those who desired or needed a period of spiritual purification. Restitution and spiritual cleansing would occur under the direction of kāhuna.

When I first became aware of the idea of the city of refuge, I was struck by its psychological significance. We have all been pursued by inner persecutors. Most of us know our harsh inner critic, the judge that evokes feelings of guilt far in excess our "crimes." Infractions, real or imagined, carry a life sentence. Guilt can actually be a positive emotion, a simple corrective that allows us to be in another's shoes and feel our impact on them. Or it can awaken us to how we have fallen short of our own standards. Once guilt has confronted us with our shortcoming, and we have made amends and learned from the experience, the matter is settled. Guilt falls away. People who do not experience this kind of guilt are labeled as sociopaths by modern psychology.

Yet there is another kind of guilt that has no constructive purpose. It is some of the junk in the subconscious—memories replaying endlessly. Making amends and learning are not enough for the inner critic. Its aim seems to be to make us feel as lousy about ourselves as possible. There is no appeasing it because in most cases it became firmly imbedded in Subconscious Mind during our pre-verbal childhood or even as a result of perinatal events. Therefore it does not respond well to counter-arguments or other verbal efforts to soften and subdue it. The result is that psychic energy that could be used more creatively is bound up, and our self-esteem and confidence is diminished.

The city of refuge, as an inner place, is a region of ourselves that we may not be aware of, for our western world has no equivalent external version to serve as a model. The idea that we can go within—to an area of ourselves from which the tyrant judge/critic is denied entry—is of profound significance from the vantage of emotional healing. That within this place, there is an agency of mind that conducts a process to make us *pono*—right with ourselves and with the world to which we will return. The puʻuhonua as an inner domain is a capacity that is, in effect, hardwired into our psychological makeup. But unlike the fight or flight reaction, which is instant and automatic, it has to be consciously activated. The computer comes from the factory with the program installed, but we have to learn how to use it. We come from the factory already assembled to do the Hoʻoponopono process, but we need instruction.

Perhaps in anger, I have said something that offends you, something caustic and uncharacteristic of the way I relate to people. It hurts you and startles us both. Though I am upset with myself and I'm also hurting for you, at the same time I feel that my anger was justified—though perhaps not to the degree I felt and expressed it. Such a confusing conglomeration of feelings is often the occasion for nasty self-judgments to enter the fray.

The first task is to get our head above water enough in this stormy sea so we can recognize what is happening, for a psychological event is building that is more than the simple tiff that set it off. This recognition that allows us to perceive that we have a problem also makes it possible to stop momentarily and to choose to make an inward journey to the puʻuhonua.

One approach is to go through a relaxation procedure and then to visualize a safe haven in your mind's eye. It might be a familiar place in which you felt safe and secure and at peace, or it might be a place that exists solely in your imagination. As you evoke the details of the place—colors, textures, temperature, breezes, fragrances, you can enter its refuge and begin a detailed healing ritual process by first acknowledging the error—directed toward the person offended, toward yourself, and/or your higher power. You request forgiveness from any person, part of self, or Divinity you sense has been offended by your act. To complete the process, you ask that this whole matter now be laid to rest and that the emotional energy that had been bound by it be released for the good of all concerned.

To whom or what is the request made? This depends upon your beliefs. For some it could be God or Jesus, others may prefer "High Self" or Higher Power or some personal variation. What is important is invoking an inner agency with greater power for good than your offending limited self. To follow up, you might choose to make amends with the person on the receiving end of your misdeed. Interestingly, people who have gone through this inner process often report that the other person has been unexpectedly receptive to the amends—or has even dismissed the whole affair as a fluke.

A Three Stage Process

The clearing of psychological material that presents itself as a problem involves three elements—repentance, forgiveness and transmutation. First, the error must be acknowledged. The act of regarding it as an error is an act of contrition, perhaps including "I'm sorry." Then forgiveness for the commission of the error is sought. Finally, the error and everything that has ridden in on it from the subconscious warehouse is transmuted to a state of neutrality. This frees the energy that has been bound up in it to be used for inspired, creative, and loving thought, feeling and actions in the world.

Such a visualization might indeed rectify the situation in question, so that both the relationship and the offender's psyche are left free of residual thoughts or feelings pushed into the Subconscious Mind. It can (but does not necessarily) address whatever unconscious material created or amplified the disharmony in the first place. If this sort of behavior seems to be a pattern, psychological techniques have been developed to address the unconscious roots. If the specific example is healed without healing the underlying problem, variations on the same theme will recur repeatedly.

In the old Hawaiian system, once a person entered the puʻuhonua, they could not be arrested. When they came out, they were regarded as free and clear of their offenses. Their slate was clean. The energy tied up in the offense was, in effect, transmuted to zero. The energy of forgiveness was thoroughly embraced in that institution.

The critical elements of the visualization protocol—repentance, forgiveness, and transmutation—are the defining elements of the Ho'oponopono process termed *cleaning*. Yet Ho'oponopono differs from visualization and a host of other psychological techniques, in that cleaning is a much more immediately accessible process. Cleaning works at the level of the memory itself and not its cognitive and behavioral manifestations.

This is no small factor for our overly busy, over-committed western lives—with no lines left blank on the to-do list. We can practice the cleaning process ongoingly. It will transform the attention we typically give to stress-producing thinking into a process of deep inner healing. The Ho'oponopono process allows us to reside in the pu'uhonua even while engaging in life, as it continues to neutralize all life-limiting influences.

The Ho'oponopono process also works at the level of the deep unconscious to dissolve the factors that created the problem. This consciously initiated process can heal psychological problems at a fundamental, unconscious level even in the background of daily activities. In our contemporary culture, we tend to believe that for something to be effective it has to be complicated and difficult, requiring the ongoing intervention of an expert. Instead, this is a practice that invites us to view each moment as an opportunity to liberate ourselves *and* the world, and gives us the tools we need. Thus we gradually erase the memories that habitually replay—to the distress of ourselves and the world—and allow the Divine to enter where memories once lodged. As both a problem-solving process and a way of life, rather than requiring more time of us, it redirects the mental activity involved in the way we normally spend our time.

To understand the dynamic operation of this structure, let's say our rainmaker is a Ho'oponopono practitioner. As he surveys the drought scenario, he might see the parched land, feel the dry air, hear the fears and sufferings of the people—so that he might experience all this as a problem. When his experience moves from being an unconditional acceptance of things exactly as they are in the present moment to reacting to a problem, it is a sure sign that in the Subconscious Mind memories are replaying.

Acceptance does not mean condoning or approving. It simply means being fully present to the situation as it presents itself, without judgment or agenda. To be in acceptance is to be in Tao—in Ho'oponopono language, to be at Zero. Memories replaying define the situation as a problem. So we are no longer at Zero, no longer in Tao, no longer "being in the ordinance of heaven." By cleaning the memories replaying that are manifesting as drought and defining the drought as a problem, we empty the rocks from our Bowl of Light. The cleaning tool is saying on our behalf, "I'm sorry, Divine Creator, for errors (memories) in me that are showing up as this problem. Please forgive me for these errors, and please transmute them to zero so that the universe will be free of them."

The Dynamics of Cleaning

Cleaning begins with the Conscious Mind or 'Uhane. Conscious Mind is viewed in a derogatory light by some spiritual practitioners because it is seen as the domain of Ego. For them it stands in the way of an enlightened perspective, perhaps even something to be eradicated. Ego is indeed problematic if it has enthroned itself as the agency of mind that speaks with highest authority on the nature of reality, using the faculty of the intellect as the only tool to comprehend reality. Norretranders' observations suggest that this is an inflated view at odds with the facts. A Conscious Mind that sees itself as such a center of power is undoubtedly one possessed by memories replaying, though clueless to this occurring. It sees its explanatory and problem-solving power as unassailable.

Jim Nourse, PhD

What various mystical traditions seem to be saying is that the map that the intellect fashions should not be mistaken for the territory to which it refers. What is being presented in this book, for example, is an ego-mind, intellectual description of the Hoʻoponopono process—a map. The only importance of this material is to serve as encouragement and guidance into the process itself. ʻUhane, having read and understood the map, is the agency of mind that chooses to engage the practice. As ʻUhane we must remember to do it, choose to do it, and cultivate a consistent practice. The use of a cleaning tool is not unlike a meditative focus that diverts the mind from its customary chatter, which is mostly mental confusion masquerading as problem-solving.

Once the cleaning process is initiated by the Conscious Mind, a remarkable process unfolds, graphically shown in Figure 3.

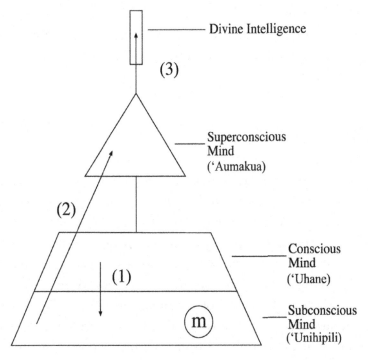

Figure 3. Initiation of cleaning process

A flow of mana is activated which can be regarded as an energetic petition to the Divine, a call for support (1). This flow, however, is not a direct flow from conscious mind to the Divine. There are two thresholds that must be passed first. 'Unihipili, the Subconscious Mind, must be on board and not opposed to the conscious decision to clean. Someone whose conscious wish is to get a better job or find a fulfilling relationship, but who feels unconsciously unworthy, will find efforts to manifest a positive change ineffective.

One aspect of 'Unihipili is like what psychologist John Bradshaw described as an "inner child." If our inner child is bound by shame and fear or by a conviction of being bad, she cannot feel worthy of approaching Divinity—much less of receiving the desired gifts of Divinity. Consequently a significant portion of the training in Ho'oponopono is devoted to working with enlisting 'Unihipili as an ally.

If 'Unihpili is in accord with the cleaning, it takes the petition to 'Aumakua, the Superconscious Mind, that is in direct proximity to the Divine (2). 'Aumakua has the ability to see the big picture, to reflect our highest potential, and is broad and deep enough to discern the highest good. It reviews what is presented by 'Unihipili from its higher perspective. Then 'Aumakua offers to Divinity a petition for the highest good (3).

That Subconscious Mind can act as either obstruction or conduit to the Divine is a profound psychological truth. The spiritual realm opens fully to us only when we do the necessary work with the subconscious. The spiritual life suffers or prospers to the degree that our psychological nature is *pono*, that is, balanced and in harmony.

At the level of 'Aumakua, Self and Divine are One. When the energetic petition has been clarified at the level of 'Aumakua, it is "as it should be by the ordinance of Heaven," and proceeds to Divinity which begins the transmutational process illustrated in Figure 4.

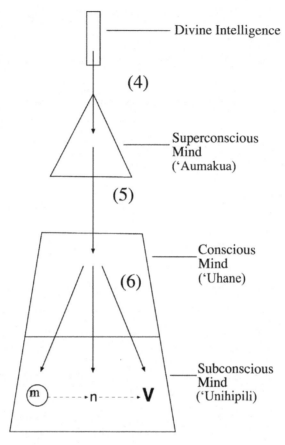

Figure 4. Completion of the Cleaning Process

The descent of cleansing mana from the Divine is now activated, flowing down through the strata of mind, Superconscious (4), Conscious (5) and Subconscious (6). Arriving at Subconscious Mind, the mana erases the memory (m) that was generating the problematic experience, neutralizing its energy (n) and leaves a condition of Void (V), the pristine state of the mind, in the space previously occupied by the memory. This opens the opportunity for Divine Inspiration to enter the area vacated by the memory.

When a harmonious relationship between conscious and subconscious is achieved, the Ho'oponopono process can reconcile us with our problematic aspects. As Superconscious Mind refines our mental content to align with the highest good of self and others, the Ho'oponopono process can reconcile us with the Divine. The downward, then upward, then downward flow of mana, and the energetic alignment that ensues on all *four* levels—subconscious, conscious, superconscious, and Divinity—I call The *Aloha* Mind.

Aloha Mind is a mind at Zero. While the word *Aloha* means Love, and is used as a traditional greeting, it is a richly nuanced word. It is a synthesis of alo "in the presence of" and ha "breath," viewed by Hawaiians (as in many cultures) as Divine spirit, in-spir-ation, the indwelling spirit of Divinity. When I say *Aloha* to you, I am saying that I recognize the Divine in you and that we are one in the presence of the Divine. It is both a greeting, a blessing, and an acknowledgement of the fundamental reality of the cosmos.

Aloha Mind is mind occupied by Divinity on all levels. It is rainmaker mind.

Each time a cleaning process is initiated, there is an instant of *Aloha*-mindedness. As cleaning is adopted as a way of life, so that all experience is viewed as opportunity for cleaning, Divine Inspiration increasingly occupies the spaces where memories replayed. Thus we become more fully established in *Aloha* Mind.

Cleaning Tools

The tools that are used in the practice of Ho'oponopono are words, phrases, visualizations, and actions that embody the processes of repentance, forgiveness, and transmutation. Condensed within each of these tools is the energetic message "I'm sorry, Divine Creator, for errors (memories) that occur in me that give rise to this problem. Please forgive me for these errors, and please transmute them to zero so that the universe will be free from them." Each tool stimulates an energetic petition to the Divine to erase memories and substitute Inspiration, as the cleaning tools themselves are products of Inspiration. There are core tools, in use for many years, that are given to participants in Ho'oponopono classes. In addition, a part of the instruction concerns the acquisition of our own personal cleaning tools.

The tool that has been most widely circulated is the simple phrase "I love you." In the beginning, it is typically engaged when we're experiencing some problem—an uncomfortable emotion, a relationship conflict, an upsetting news report, a physical or medical challenge, anything that strikes us as disturbing. In thinking "I love you" repeatedly, it is important to recognize that this phrase is a tool—not unlike a screwdriver. When we are fastening two boards together with a wood screw, we do not require passion to enter the act; we need not pay homage to Henry F. Phillips for the screw nor the screwdriver that he invented. It might be a nice thing to do, but it is not required for the operation to be a success. As Mabel Katz has noted, we do not need to hit the delete button on the computer with any fervor for it to perform the desired action. The effectiveness of "I love you"—or any healing tool—is not dependent on formally setting an intention, conjuring an emotion congruent with the intention, nor visualizing a desired outcome.

Yet historically we have spoken such words in the presence of a deeply felt emotion. It is thus likely that the words have associative links to positive subconscious emotional content. I and others have noticed that the unconscious feeling of love can become conscious during the cleaning process (even if it was not initially present), yet it is not a requirement for the process to work.

Dr. Hew Len has said we really don't know what the heck is going on in ourselves and in the Cosmos at any given moment, so it is actually wise to be continuously engaging the cleaning process. Though we are likely to begin using it when we have become aware of a problem, it is easy to be thinking the phrase subvocally throughout the day. This is much easier than it might seem. After the Conscious Mind repeatedly decides to initiate the cleaning process, it becomes habitual in the background of thought—for it is actually picked up by ʻUnihipili which then promotes the cleaning process subconsciously, even when we are sleeping. As ʻUhane and ʻUnihipili form an alliance and co-engage this process, the practice is greatly strengthened.

Not all tools are verbal, and this is nicely illustrated by Blue Solar Water. Fresh Water (*wai*, in Hawaiian) is viewed as a sacred substance, which makes sense as it is the basis of life. (Corresponding practices in other traditions acknowledge the healing qualities of specially treated water—for example, water blessed by a priest becoming holy water). In Hoʻoponopono practice, water that has been placed in a blue bottle and set in the sun is regarded as having the ability to evoke the cleaning process. Used for drinking, cooking, cleaning, bathing, Blue Solar Water operates non-verbally to promote the entire process just described.

Our cat, who had been diagnosed with kidney failure, had begun drinking copious quantities of water as his disease worsened. When given the choice between regular water and Blue Solar Water he would invariably go for the Blue Solar Water. He lived well beyond the veterinarian's predictions.

Another commonly used cleaning tool is "Thank You." This phrase can express the attitude of receptivity and gratitude, which is the essence of spiritual life. It says that whatever comes my way—no matter whether Conscious Mind evaluates it as pleasant or unpleasant—is a gift, and my life will be greatly enriched by recognizing the gift, cultivating the skill to relate to it, and using it in a wise and compassionate way. To use "Thank You" as a cleaning tool does not require this elaboration. However, the very decision to clean is a decision to accept what comes, take responsibility and not be hijacked by whatever stream of thinking and emotion habitually has dominated us.

By erasing the memories that keep us stuck and allowing Divine Inspiration to take their place, the cleaning process itself begins to render the feeling tones and thought patterns inherent in "I Love You" and "Thank You." This is not faking it 'til you make it. This is taking responsibility, letting go, and letting God. What then becomes possible is genuine Love and genuine Gratitude.

He kēhau hoʻomaʻemaʻe ke Aloha

Aloha is like a cleansing dew

CHAPTER EIGHT

Ho'oponopono, Psychotherapy and Healing

Helpful Being, then, is the goal.
What we have to offer others
will come from our sense of unity.
So we look for and cherish
those experiences in which we feel ourselves
connected to all things in the universe.

Ram Dass

One of the reasons cleaning is so important is that there is simply no way to clear out the subconscious region of mind through a process of verbal analysis. Conventional insight-oriented psychotherapy—to its credit—has recognized that problems have unconscious determinants. For any given course of therapy it is not necessary to bring everything out of the basement for examination. But I am sobered when working with a patient who announces in exasperation, "but I thought I dealt with all my mother issues with my last therapist!" There are different ways of explaining why we return so often to the same material. Conscious Mind by itself—even conscious mind having unearthed unconscious material and achieved healing insight—seems to fall short of the full and lasting resolution we wish for.

Even if the process of making the unconscious conscious were dizzyingly effective, Ho'oponopono practice is much broader. Memories replaying in the Subconscious Mind do not just create emotional and physical problems. They create much of the whole complex of experience that we call reality. All that we experience as our world is the product of our perception. Is this perception clear—characterized by a mind empty of these memories—or is it distorted by the ongoing replaying of data bits below the level of our conscious awareness? If we are serious about emptying all the rocks from the Bowl of Light, cleaning needs to be ongoing, the melody playing in the background of experience.

Dr. Hew Len's experience at Hawai'i State Hospital offers a profound and dramatic example of how ongoing cleaning of memories by processes of repentance, forgiveness and transmutation *performed on oneself* can change the surrounding world. My experience confirms this phenomenon, though an outpatient practice is naturally a less-controlled environment.

Our professional experience might suggest that psychotherapy, or any other procedure, is not needed if the clinician is doing the Ho'oponopono process. This may be true, but people seeking help expect to be treated in a certain fashion, so healers and psychotherapists must operate in the appropriate context.

In my training in psychoanalytic theory I was taught to be aware of my own reactions to the patient and make use of them diagnostically, while considering what reactions might be reflective of my own neuroses. I was of a generation of therapists for whom receiving our own therapy was essentially all but mandatory, precisely because it was recognized that un-treated therapists would be seeing patients through the lens of their own problems. So, while the therapy I have practiced most of my career certainly takes self into account, it does so to facilitate an undistorted focus on the patient.

At the first Hoʻoponopono class I attended, Dr. Hew Len had been talking about the problem of psychotherapist burnout, stemming from the fact that psychotherapy was all about trying to change someone else—when all one can do is change oneself. He was quite adamant. During a break I wanted to argue that psychotherapy does not try to change anyone, but shows people where they are stuck and, in some systems, how to get unstuck.

Much of the training in psychotherapy today is in short term techniques preferred by insurance and pharmaceutical companies, which place all the focus not on what is going on *in* the patient, but on the patient's *functioning*. The new techniques are the epitome of other-focused approaches. To practice these techniques it probably would not be good if the therapist were psychotic, but they certainly do not need the level of self-knowledge required for depth psychotherapy. This discussion might well be confusing to anyone not privy to the intrigues of the professional psychotherapy world, asking "How could psychotherapy *not* be other-focused? After all, isn't the purpose of psychotherapy to help the patient? Do I want to see a therapist who is spending my whole session working on herself?"

The correct answer is "Yes, you do."

Dr. Hew Len successfully "treated" the patients at Hawaiʻi State Hospital solely by working on himself. While I would agree that "working on myself" is a good practice in psychotherapy, this psychologist clearly meant something different by the phrase than I was used to. This was not a process of sorting thorough my own psyche to discover the origins of my reactions and disentangle them from the task of the moment, but rather was a radical act of taking full and complete responsibility for everything in my experience of this moment. If it is in my experience, it is in me—and it is mine to heal.

This means that when you come to me as a patient and begin to tell your story, your story and all that goes with it become mine. If that's all there were to it, I would indeed be burned out in very short order. Responsibility in this context does not mean blame, nor does it mean burden. It is more of the nature of an assignment. And the assignment is not given without the tools to be used to undertake it.

Whenever something enters the field of my awareness that I experience as a problem, I can be certain that what is occurring is memories replaying. As long as memories are replaying, I am stuck, you are stuck, the universe is stuck. To clear the memories I must engage the process of repentance, forgiveness and transmutation. In effect, I am saying "I am sorry, Divine Creator, for errors in me that are manifesting as John's depression. Please forgive me for these errors, and please transmute them to Zero." It is not my job to transmute the problem to Zero—only Divinity can do that. But I have to initiate the process with one or more of the cleaning tools. I have to remember to do this, and I have to use my desire to help you as a signal to put my attention into using the tools. Responsibility does not mean that I try to fix you or save you—or even sympathize with you. I *can* sympathize and be caring, and do things. I can give you an umbrella if it's raining and I can give you the benefit of my counsel, which you may find helpful—but if I really want to help at the level of the very foundation of the problem, I bring it all back inside and work on myself using the cleaning process.

From the Ho'oponopono perspective this is actually anything but burdensome. In fact, it is an occasion for gratitude, because your situation gives me the opportunity to clean out my own subconscious warehouse, setting me, you, and everyone else free in the process.

Aloha is a power that erases all divisions between people, between people and nature, between a person and him/herself. When I am in *Aloha* Mind I know that, while I may not be having the same experience as you, the seed, the data point, the memory that is now giving rise to your depression is the same seed that gives rise to suffering in me, whatever its particular manifestation might be.

With anything that you experience, the possibility for it exists in me also. It is said that we all have the potential to be Hitlers under the right combinations of circumstances—or to be saints. The stones of memory or the Light of Inspiration are the same in all of us. When using the cleaning tools, which embody repentance and forgiveness, I am acknowledging that, though you have brought me the story of your suffering, the seed of that same suffering is in my subconscious. I can say, through the cleaning process, "I'm sorry, Divine Creator, please forgive me," not because I am guilty or condemned or evil, but because I am human. What you bring me that seems to be yours alone is in me already, and you have blessed me with a reminder. You may be called patient and I may be called doctor, but these are only the conventions by which we live and the roles our destinies have assigned to us. I am no better nor of a higher station than you. How can I presume to heal you? In *Aloha*, I come to the Divine acknowledging that I bear within me the same error that has led to your suffering. When I engage in repentance and ask for forgiveness, these are not the actions of a shamed and humiliated person on a guilt trip. These are expressions of the power of *Aloha*, offered with the conviction that they link directly to and evoke the third energy, transmutation—which is Divinity's answer.

My conclusion after practicing Ho'oponopono is that my patients enjoy considerable benefit from the work I consistently do on myself. I am most astonished by the positive changes made in difficult cases for which the prognosis was initially poor. An elderly gentleman with crippling low back pain that by all rights should have taken months to heal but was, by his own estimate, 90% improved with one acupuncture treatment. An individual, unamenable to psychotherapy, in short order was undergoing a depth analysis of core conflicts and making peace in his marriage. A highly rational agnostic experienced a spontaneous unitive spiritual state which was transformational. There are many more examples, yet my purpose here is not to tout or promote my practice but to indicate that there are experiences in my professional sphere that are convincing enough to me that I would consider it a disservice to my patients, let alone to myself, to cease this inner work.

There are also individuals who have not achieved the results they desire during our time together. While I long ago abandoned the idea that everyone would leave my office healed and satisfied, it is my belief that the cleaning of memories which occurred during their time as my patient, while not manifesting in symptom resolution, has lessened the power that maintains these symptoms. When I remember such a person, I treat it as an opportunity to continue to clean with the memory.

I may never know whether they have benefitted. They may have moved on to another practitioner and had more satisfactory results. Is this because he was a better clinician, or had a better approach, or the relationship was a better "fit," or the timing was right, or the motivation better? Who can know for sure? I worked with an individual whose emotional life was restricted mostly to anger. He returned after a long hiatus to describe a much expanded repertoire of feeling. Was it time, was it intervening experience, was it a biochemical shift? Or was it the cleaning process that emptied the bowl of stones at just the right time. There is no way to prove any of these contentions, neither the conventional explanations nor the Ho'oponopono process. What I realize now is that getting stuck on trying to figure out what cannot ultimately be decided by thinking is itself an expression of memories replaying. It is a misappropriation of thought.

It is only at the level of Divinity that an outcome that is *pono* is known. While I may be supportive of the patient in his desire for a certain outcome, it is important that I remember that neither I nor the patient know what outcome is ultimately in his best interests nor those he affects. This allows me to relax with my patient. The cleaning process allows me to stay focused and be more present, more patient and more honoring of the Light in his bowl.

Therapist burnout is quite common in my profession. Though we are taught about taking care of ourselves, even when we do our best by the nature of the profession we end up taking on a lot that we cannot easily release. The new name for it is *compassion fatigue*. It sets in because we misconstrue responsibility. It is not just that our patients expect us to fix them or rescue them, and that we get hooked by unconscious power and rescue fantasies that our own analysis did not altogether eradicate, or that the legal system expects us to take responsibility for our patients' lives, not just their therapy. We do not have a moment-to-moment Divinely assisted self-cleaning process that allows us to metabolize the memories being activated in real time—and in such great volume and frequency—during a therapy session that no amount of psychoanalytic self-scrutiny can handle the load, and we are left with a heavy residue.

The Ho'oponopono process offers a way for therapists to take responsibility that is inherently healing to both patient and therapist. This does not mean that the work is quick and easy. But it does mean that responsibility does not have to be burdensome.

This insight is not restricted to the therapist/client or doctor/patient relationship. Although formalized in such relationships, helping is one of the things we do at various times in nearly all relationships, and at times this can become formidable. Just ask anyone caring for a family member with Alzheimer's. But even in less demanding situations—a friend going through a rough spot in life and needing emotional support—we can take on the other's suffering and feel overwhelmed by the responsibility. Knowing that these scenarios are memories replaying and armed with the Ho'oponopono process, we are empowered to call upon a higher wisdom that allows Divinity both to be in charge of outcomes and to fashion the quality of our presence to be inherently healing.

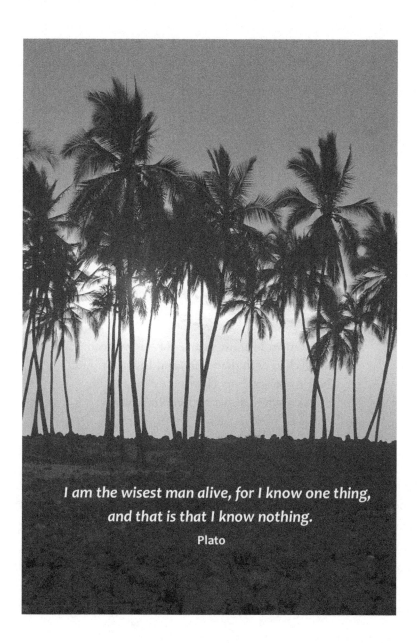

I am the wisest man alive, for I know one thing,
and that is that I know nothing.

Plato

CHAPTER NINE

Creating the Life of Your Dreams

My crown is in my heart, not on my head;
Not decked with diamonds and Indian stones,
Nor to be seen: my crown is called content:
A crown it is that seldom kings enjoy.

Henry VI, Part 3, Act. 3, Scene 1
William Shakespeare

The ability to visualize our desires, set goals and plan for their achievement is a key feature of being human. The human-made aspect of the world around us—houses, gardens, skyscrapers, countries, the internet—all began as ideas in someone's mind. From what we have learned about Ho'oponopono, to what degree are these creations the products of Divine Inspiration? Or of memories replaying?

It is unlikely that the state of the world as we see it today is wholly the product of Divine Inspiration. Regardless of our achievements as individuals, and even as a species, our best efforts inevitably yield unanticipated consequences. We attain our desires but the part of us that desires is not satisfied—it just hands us a new list. We suffer when do not get what we want. When we do get it, we suffer from our efforts to hang onto it or from the pressure to get even more.

Not until we have dealt with the inner promptings themselves can we see that no amount of manipulation of the outer world will satisfy them. This question, of course, is not new. Contemplative traditions over many centuries have offered this wisdom to a sleeping humanity that seems to remain steadfast in its slumber. Yet the fact that such traditions remain alive despite their few adherents suggests that they speak truths that we are disposed to hear and take seriously.

In recent years we have seen a flood of instructional material on how to create states of consciousness that will "magnetize" or attract what or whom we desire. Probably the best known source of the philosophy and technique of manifestation is *The Secret,* originally released as a film in 2006 and subsequently as a book. Its ideas have precedents in various treatments of *The Law of Attraction* described by theosophical writers and in material channeled by Esther Hicks. Their fundamental prescription is to create a clear internal visualization of what is desired, to *feel* it as already having been obtained, and to experience gratitude that it has been given. In this view, it is the grateful experience of a desired outcome as something that already exists in the here and now that attracts that reality into our life. This approach is in contrast to petitionary prayer—asking God to deliver something that we currently lack or to create an outcome different from the present state of affairs. Proponents of the Law of Attraction would maintain that the feeling of lack or of aversion toward the present situation—what characterizes the emotional foundation of much prayer—will attract more of what is *not* desired.

The most frequently heard criticism of *The Secret* is its focus on using the Law of Attraction to secure material gratification. It can certainly be used to attract higher states of being, but this is not its contemporary emphasis. The focus on material abundance reflects not only a misguided faith in materialistic solutions to psychospiritual problems, but also in the ability of the Conscious Mind to choose wisely. If we remove this materialist bias, what most of us desire is peace of mind, equanimity, love, security, wisdom and other sublime states of experience that are not dependent on or defined by external conditions. We should not confuse what we want with what is necessary to bring us there.

In large part these misconceptions are supported by a *monopsychic* view of mind—mind as essentially a single, independent entity and whose conscious aspect is the most important determinant of what we regard as our reality. While mention might be made of subconscious factors, little or no attention is given to dealing with their capacity to assist or obstruct conscious intention. The whole effort is aimed at configuring Conscious Mind in such a way that desired results will manifest.

As we have seen, the Hawaiian conception of mind regards Conscious Mind as but one part of a three-part structure. While it is equipped with an impressive array of capabilities, these assets are easily commandeered by subconscious factors. We, as Conscious Mind, cannot simply override or overwrite these factors, for they are too subtle and too powerful. Therefore, what we conceive to accomplish without dealing with them will carry their taint, and whatever we manage to attract will reflect their influence.

Additionally, Superconscious Mind recognizes that Conscious Mind, even when relatively unhampered by memories replaying, has a limited perspective. Being always in a state of communion with Divinity, it is likewise concerned with the greater good and with creating experiences that serve the highest evolutionary potential of the individual. It is profoundly beyond the ability of Conscious Mind to orchestrate an experience that is the complex coalescence of these factors.

Both Hoʻoponopono and contemporary interpretations of the Law of Attraction advocate taking full responsibility for one's life. To decide to take full responsibility is powerful—and one that lies solely in the hands of Conscious Mind. These approaches differ in their pathways: The Law of Attraction instructs Conscious Mind to visualize and manifest, while Hoʻoponopono instructs Conscious Mind to let go and let God.

Through the practice of cleaning, what Conscious Mind desires, conceives and works toward is progressively freed from the influence of memories replaying and informed by the influence of Divine Inspiration. It is not that I stop desiring, striving, or creating. It is that the "I" that is doing it is the "I" of Aloha Mind, which is Divinity infusing the process. Conscious mind is a participant in the art of making a reality that is right and perfect for me and for all, rather than having to figure it all out by itself and making huge moves with far-reaching consequences based on the terribly inadequate information at its disposal.

We have all experienced ourselves as victims rather than heroes in our own stories. The idea that we can employ a procedure to create a more desirable reality comes as a blessing when we are in a period of adversity or just tired of the same old dissatisfactions. In this respect, both the Law of Attraction and the Hoʻoponopono process offer ways of becoming active participants in the restructuring of our lives. The redefinition of our stance toward life from passive to active itself produces a feeling of enhanced well-being.

The sort of activity that characterizes the contemporary use of the Law of Attraction is what I would characterize as active assertiveness—knowing what I want, building a mental and emotional impetus behind it, and claiming it with gratitude. By contrast, the Hoʻoponopono process may seem passive, that the Conscious Mind is giving up and stepping aside. Not so at all. The activity that characterizes the Hoʻoponopono process is much more the nature of a martial artist or meditation master. Neither passivity nor assertiveness, the Hoʻoponopono process cultivates a stance of *active receptivity*. It says, "I know what I want, but I am willing to acknowledge that I don't know if that is best for me and all concerned, so I choose to initiate a process that will help me get clear and provide me with what is right and perfect for myself and for the world."

Just as we have all had the experience of being victims, we have also experienced "things working out for the best," even though at first we would have changed the situation if we could. The Ho'oponopono process implicitly holds that Conscious Mind is incapable of providing adequate solutions to the problems it encounters. Its domain is that of a short-sighted lesser story, so its solutions will give at best temporary relief because they are all creations of the lesser story.

The promise Ho'oponopono holds forth is that there is a greater story, a Great Work, known to Superconscious Mind/Divinity that becomes manifest as Conscious Mind relaxes, cleans, and releases.

There *is* a law of attraction implicit in the Ho'oponopono process, but it is not that of the conscious personality attempting to dictate to the Universe the terms of its satisfaction. What is attracted is Divinity. The problems created in the small story can only be solved, and the life desired can only be lived, when we allow the greater story to be realized.

The hero of the greater story is not limited to having done what he has set out to do in the material world. More importantly, he is one who has achieved a high level of mastery of *himself*, who is not overrun by memories replaying, who takes responsibility for his experience moment to moment, and who permits himself, with humility, to be instructed by an intelligence higher than his own conscious understanding. This is hero as *Kahuna*. Whether we are known by that name or by no particular title at all, the path that leads us toward a full realization of who we are is ultimately of greater value to us than is the satisfaction of a craving. The Ho'oponopono path may yield disappointment when a wished-for outcome is not achieved, but offers a way to use even the disappointment as an assist rather an obstacle.

There is a story of a novice meditation student having a hideous series of meditations involving all sorts of negative thoughts and images. Convinced he is doing something wrong, he approaches his teacher— who laughs and tells him to just let it go. Thereafter he has a series of wonderful meditations with bliss and peace. Convinced he has now gotten it right, he reports his success to the master—who laughs and tells him to just let it go. The mastery we are talking about here is one that evokes a peace with life on its own terms, from a high perspective that is unruffled either by getting what we want or what we don't want.

Established in this heightened awareness, we are rainmakers, and the snow falls because Divinity has a better idea.

Ua mau ke ea o ka ʻāina, i ka pono

CHAPTER TEN

A Final Word About Pono

Ua mau ke ea o ka 'āina, i ka pono

The life of the land is perpetuated in righteousness

Thus says the official motto of the state of Hawai'i. I first heard these Hawaiian words in a song called "Hawai'i '78," written by Mickey Ioane and performed by Israel Kamakawiwo'ole, beloved vocalist, ukuleleist and composer. If you ever hear the music of Israel, Braddah Iz, you will immediately know that if souls have size, this is a big, big soul. When I first heard the standard translation of this motto, something about it seemed out of sync with what I was hearing in this powerful song.

The customary translation brought to my mind Grant Wood's painting, American Gothic. The word "righteous," while inherently neutral, referring to a positive moral and ethical attitude, has acquired over the years a theological connotation suggestive of a certain rigidity or inflexibility in determining what is or is not pleasing to God. While those of some religious persuasions may have no problem with this, something about this translation does not reflect what I have come to understand about the Hawaiian world view.

When I asked Kopa what was the true meaning of *pono*, his first reply was, "what does it mean to you, Jim?" Spoken like a psychotherapist! He wanted to begin from the vantage of my own level of understanding. I replied, "balance." "Yes, it can mean that. It can also mean"—he then placed his hand on Judith's forehead. She had been contending with a sinus infection—"healed, made well . . . *pono*! Before she was sick, now she is *pono*." He went on to say that Hawaiian words often do not have the strict, circumscribed meanings that English words have, that the speaker and listener can both impact the meaning. He indicated that *pono* is a very powerful word that suggests a state of being that is whole, present, undivided—at peace but at the same embodying great power.

From the Hawaiian Dictionary: "Goodness, uprightness, morality, moral qualities, correct or proper procedure, excellence, well-being, prosperity, welfare, benefit, behalf, equity, sake, true condition or nature, duty; moral, fitting, proper, righteous, right, upright, just, virtuous, fair, beneficial, successful, in perfect order, accurate, correct, eased, relieved; should, ought, must, necessary." A range of meanings that includes morality/righteousness is acknowledged, but it is clear that the word cannot be reduced to such a notion.

The use of the word in the state motto has historical, political and spiritual significance. In 1843, in response to claims that British residents had suffered various political abuses, the King, persuaded by the captain of the HMS Carysfort and its firepower, ceded the Kingdom of Hawai'i to Great Britain. After he managed to inform London of the captain's actions, sovereignty was ceded back to the King. Shortly thereafter, the king gave a speech at Kawaiha'o Church, where he is said to have spoken the words which later became the state motto. Kamehameha III had been raised in the traditional Hawaiian ways but also received a Western education. It is said that he was torn between the ways of the two cultures. We cannot know for certain whether the phrase reflects the more recent missionary influence that the King had embraced, or was the reflection of a deeper notion of "rightness" more consonant with the native connection with the land and the life spirit dwelling within it—or perhaps a synthesis of the two sensibilities struggling to occur within the soul of Kamehameha III.

In this light, ponder these alternate translations of the words of the state motto:

> The life of the land continues since the actions taken were proper.
> The life of the land goes on, now that things are as they should be again.
> The life of the land continues, now that things are properly ordered.
> The life force continues in nature; nature lives on and prospers, now that the king has been restored to his proper place and has resumed his nurturing relationship with it.
>
> —Michael Kioni Dudley, *Man, Gods and Nature*

The issue illustrated here is that the *ea,* the life force, is dependent upon the sovereign being in his correct place and in correct relationship with the world entrusted to his care. In applying the thematic content of this idea to the psychospiritual realm, the life force flows properly when Divinity is properly invested as the sovereign power of the individual. The Ego/Conscious Mind/Middle Self, particularly as it has evolved in the Western psyche isolated from other spheres of the total mind, has ceded to itself a power that it is inherently incapable of wielding wisely—because by virtue of its natural limitations, it lacks the ability to gauge the far-reaching consequences of its actions. Cut off from the

High Self and its connection with Divinity, it fails to perceive the vast network of interconnectedness that comprises the world on all its various levels. When usurping sovereignty, Middle Self/Conscious Mind reveals itself as ill-equipped to be in charge, prone as it is to short-sidedness, obsession with self-preservation, self-promotion, greed, and aggressive self-interest—and with its defenses that permit it to rationalize as good whatever offers satisfaction. As Dr. Hew Len says, "What does the intellect know? Nothing. What does God know? Everything."

In addition to managing the mechanics of daily living, what Middle Self/Conscious Mind can do very effectively is choose to engage the process of repentance, forgiveness and transmutation—which is no mean assignment. Without the initiation of the Middle Self, the process is merely a latent potential. Cleaning and maintaining ongoing practice is a psychospiritual discipline that involves far more than an attitude of righteousness. It is, rather, a dynamic process of choosing to engage in a vectoring of energy, mana, in such a way that every level of being becomes progressively resonant with the Divine. This is making *pono*. This is evoking *Aloha* Mind.

An understanding of pono includes balance, health, wholeness, rightness, coherence, and harmony. At a deeper level, pono is a precondition for the proper flow of the life force itself. In the case of the human psyche, it is the proper alignment of all three aspects of mind with Divinity. Divinity then has been returned to sovereignty, with Ego/Middle Self as subject. The word *ho'o* is a causative prefix that suggests the making, causing or securing of the condition described by the word that follows it. Thus, *ho'opono* is the making, causing or securing of a condition of balance, health, order, harmony, etc. In Hawaiian, the doubling of a word typically signifies the raising of the concept meant by the single word to a superlative degree. Thus, *ho'oponopono* suggests the securing of a condition of rightness, harmony, and balance with thoroughness, depth and completeness.

In traditional ho'oponopono practice, the completion of an intervention into an interpersonal conflict or problem is considered to settle the matter once and for all, for all time. In a similar fashion, the Ho'oponopono process as revisioned by Morrnah Nalamaku Simeona purports to utterly erase, not just subdue or manage, the data in the mind that contribute to the emergence of what the Conscious Mind perceives as a problem. As this erasure occurs at a level of Identity of Self and cosmos, once a datum is erased for the individual performing the cleaning process, it is simultaneously erased from the Cosmos at large.

While not dismissing the importance of action in the world, Ho'oponopono advocates that working at this foundational level within oneself simultaneously benefits the entire cosmos. In our extraverted culture, it is easy to regard outward activism as the only legitimate way to promote positive change. Ho'oponopono advocates that a correct inner practice benefits both inner and outer worlds which are, in fact, inseparable. Thus, as the individual thereby becomes *pono*, his actions in the world become more resonant with the Divine and are therefore inherently more helpful.

Despite this linguistic entertainment, the Ho'oponopono process is a modality that addresses fundamental sources of disharmony and imbalance, while restoring harmony and balance at the foundational level. Without dismissing the importance of morality and ethics, it reaches to a more fundamental level—the nature of the relationship between Self and World, Individual and Cosmos. It directs us how to potentiate the processes inherent in Nature—including our human nature—to bring them into balance and allow the Divine its sovereignty.

To move from the experience of increased and extended moments of Aloha-Mindedness—mind less dominated by memories and more by Divine Inspiration—to mind fully invested with Divinity, is the goal toward which we move in practicing the Ho'oponopono process. While our daily walk in this practice may be motivated by a desire to solve problems, the Bowl of Light parable indicates that it is not only to remove current stresses and make life a little easier, but to divest ourselves of the causes of those stuck spaces once and for all. As the Light is always there, it can eventually be experienced, fully and at all times.

What is extraordinary about our personal movement toward this alignment with Divinity is that it supports others in evolving as well. Mahayana Buddhism carries the notion of the Bodhisattva—one who, having attained full Enlightenment, elects to return to the world and work for the full Enlightenment of all beings. So the choice to practice the Hoʻoponopono process is a decision to bring liberation to all beings by taking full responsibility for memories replaying in each moment, then letting go and leaving outcome in the hands of Divinity. Aloha Mind is where we are all headed, sooner or later, so why not empty the Bowl and be done?

All people climb the same mountain.
The mountain, however, has many pathways...

EPILOGUE

Is This the Only Way?

. . . they had a story that there were many pathways
up the mountain, and from where one person walked
you could not see the view that the other person saw
from his side of the mountain. Only when you reached
the top of the mountain could you see and understand
all that the other person saw and believed.

Ho'opono
Pali Jae Lee

Whenever we find a philosophy, belief or practice that makes sense
on a deep level, and that awakens in us a feeling of truly being alive
and aligned with a higher order of Being, there is a natural wish to
share with others. If the teachings or life itself have not given us
sufficient humility, it is easy to come across, or to actually believe,
that we have the true way, or the only way, to an enlightened state
of being.

Self I-dentity Through Hoʻoponopono® is obviously one among many paths. I have yet to run across any teacher or practitioner of this method who claims that it is the only way or that one should abandon any other practice that is serving them well. For some, Hoʻoponopono is both a personal therapy to dissolve unconscious obstacles to happiness and fulfillment, and also the primary mode of spiritual practice. For others, it is a missing ingredient, the factor that catalyzes and potentiates other practices in their repertoire. For both, it is a powerful approach to solving problems.

When I spoke with Dr. Hew Len about being a psychologist, he did not tell me to quit my job because it was barking up the wrong tree. Neither did he tell me to do it the way he did it at Hawaiʻi State Hospital. Instead, he gave me a cleaning tool that would help me avoid absorbing the negative emotional energy present in the consulting room.

Morrnah Simeona's own teachings were testimony to value of being open to Truth—whatever year, make or model it happened to ride in on—and to be guided above all by one's own connection with Divinity. The fact that a method is ancient does not make it inherently correct. The fact that it is new does not make it inherently suspect or correct. All innovation begins as inspiration and must be put to the test of experience. If it is found to be of high value, it will eventually become ancient wisdom. If it retains its mana, it will be self-renewing.

Our modern culture, obsessed with the "new and improved," often creates new products and services that do not seem well grounded in a reality base. Once we highlight Inspiration as a quality flowing from the Divine, we risk giving license to any practice that someone has thought up and feels enthused about as coming from a sublime source. The final arbiter is the experience of many people over an expanse of time. But given our short time on this planet, we need to have a basis for judgment at the beginning, and we are not without resources for this task.

In my own system of appraisal, it is not enough that a system enjoy popularity. What differentiates a solid practice from a fad is that it must be grounded in something. It cannot have come about as a pure "intuition" that has no discernible connection with any existing body of knowledge. It may challenge the existing body of knowledge, but cannot be entirely discontinuous from it. Quantum physics did not arrive out of thin air. It was the result of scientists applying the accepted conventions while seeing the unthinkable that required a revisioning of the nature of reality itself. The new physics did not discard the Newtonian view, but rather placed parameters around it within a new contextual framework.

While the Inspiration given to Morrnah Simeona, and her considerable mana as a wisdom figure, comprise no small part of the creation of Self I-dentity Through Ho'oponopono®, they are not the sole credentials defining its validity and viability as a philosophy and psychospiritual practice. First, one can trace with great consistency the operation of its core defining principles of repentance, forgiveness and transmutation in its philosophical forebear, traditional ho'oponopono, establishing its cultural and tactical pedigree. Second, as an esoteric elaboration of the traditional exoteric practice, it is grounded in an archetypal duality (exoteric/esoteric) that is common in spiritual and religious practices. It is Inspiration anchored in solid ground, which alone could commend it to our consideration prior to any testimonials regarding its efficacy.

An additional factor, which has certainly commended the practice to me, is that the model of the human psyche it employs, insofar as it acknowledges the profound influence of Subconscious Mind, is one that has precedent and longstanding utility in my field. This correspondence seen in two traditions of thought that evolved independently is striking. The addition of a Superconscious Mind or High Self to the equation is satisfying to transpersonal psychologists, as is the description of the intimate relationship between subconscious and superconscious levels of mind. These issues are central to the work of transpersonal psychology.

The entire project of Self I-dentity Through Hoʻoponopono® consists of the explication of this relationship, how it plays out in daily experience, and how it can be used to solve problems in living while leading to higher states of being.

It is my hope that these thoughts and all that has preceded them will deliver your curiosity to the next level, and that you will begin to learn the full scope of this work from a trained teacher. While Hoʻoponopono is simple, it is also precise. I have attended several classes and have had email exchanges with teachers to have my questions answered and to ensure the correctness of my practice. Given my tendency to zero in on some aspects of the practice to the exclusion of others, it is helpful to be reacquainted with the full scope of the method.

How does one enlist the cooperation of Subconscious Mind, ʻUnihipili? You can use cleaning tools all day long, but if ʻUnihipili has a different agenda, the energy fails to be delivered to ʻAumakua—and transmutation will not occur. A significant portion of the training is devoted to working with ʻUnihipili to bring it on board. Often ʻUnihipili must be respectfully and lovingly encouraged to abandon habits of mind that may have once ensured emotional survival, but now stand in the way of growth. Such hindrances must be addressed thoroughly for the Hoʻoponopono process to work.

There is a collection of well elaborated tools and practices used in the cleaning process—techniques that embody and generate the dynamics of forgiveness, repentance, and transmutation. Even if it were permissible to list all of these in a book, it is not the most effective medium. The master/apprentice and teacher/student relationship has a dynamic of its own, a mana that adds something essential but indefinable to the specific content being transmitted. In that context there is also the opportunity for practice in a supportive environment, where questions can be immediately answered, insights shared, and misunderstandings averted.

The classroom environment is one that, for most of us, resonates on a broad level with 'Unihipili. The teacher in front of the room at the blackboard and we in our seats giving our attention (hopefully!) is an imprint firmly established in early childhood as a venue for learning something new. It is certainly not the only venue, but for most of us it was the central one. 'Unihipili likes familiarity, so we are well served if we make our initial foray into this new practice as comfortable as possible to 'Unihipili. For those who had negative experiences in the classroom, the positive attention given to 'Unihipili may itself bring about healing.

What you have in this book is an abbreviated map—and the map is not the territory. The territory is your own experience. May it be an experience rich in healing, growth, and *Aloha*. See you on the mountain!

E ALA Ē!

O KA MALUHIA NO ME OE!

AWAKEN!

PEACE BE WITH YOU!

IMAGES OF HAWAI'I

The following is a list of the photographs that appear at the beginning of each chapter:

CHAPTER HEADINGS – Nā Pali Coast, Kaua'i

INTRODUCTION – Limahuli Garden, Kaua'i

CHAPTER ONE – Wai'anae coast, O'ahu

CHAPTER TWO – Polihale Beach, Kaua'i, with Ni'ihau Island on horizon

CHAPTER THREE – Kē'ē Beach, Kaua'i. The ubiquitous wild chicken population of Kaua'i consists of descendents of those brought with the original Polynesian migrations, interbred with barnyard species raised in pens and coops throughout the island. The several hurricanes that have visited Kaua'i, and the lack of natural predators, have set them free to roam the land.

CHAPTER FOUR - One of 88 shrines at the Lāwa'i International Center, Kaua'i. The Center exists as a "gathering place for all people to hear what is not said, to see what cannot be seen, to feel what cannot be touched, to know peace...where individuals from all parts of the world can get in touch with the vestiges of their spiritual and cultural roots and traditions." www.lawaicenter.org

CHAPTER FIVE – Nā Pali coast, Kaua'i

GLOSSARY

This glossary is provided for those who wish to begin an exploration of the meanings and pronunciations of the Hawaiian words used in this book. While no written pronunciation key will address the nuances found in the spoken language, this section is meant help those who might find the Hawaiian words daunting.

Hawaiian was not originally a written language. Its rendering into written form was largely the project of American Protestant missionaries in the early nineteenth century. In the section *On Translating into Hawaiian*, the 1986 edition of the Hawaiian Dictionary quips, *He ala ehu aku kēnā* (A misty pathway, that!). The authors note that Hawaiian has more words with multiple meanings than almost any language.

Hawaiian has only thirteen letters. The consonants are **h, k, l, m, n, p, w** and **'**, the latter called the 'okina (oh-KEE-nah). All the consonants with the exception of the **w** and the 'okina are pronounced mostly the same as in English, whereas the **w** in various contexts may be pronounced as a w or a v.

The 'okina has been called a *glottal stop*, similar to the sound between the oh's in *oh-oh*. The vowels are the same as in English—**a, e, i, o, u** —but pronounced ah, eh, ee, oh, oo. In addition, one will notice a line—macron—over some vowels, which signifies that the sound is held slightly longer. A more comprehensive and precise delineation of pronunciation may be found in the Hawaiian Dictionary just referenced (see Recommended Reading).

References to possible deeper or esoteric meanings are the subject of debate in both native and academic Hawaiian circles. However, they do have standing among various philosophers and practitioners of mystical spiritual approaches that claim Hawaiian roots. For example, Morrnah Nalamaku Simeona and Hale Kealohalani Makua, both native Hawaiian kāhuna, make use of these esoteric/mystical understandings.

ʻĀina (AYE-nah) – land, earth.

Akua (ah-KOO-ah) – god, goddess, God, spirit.

Aliʻi (ah-LEE-ee) – chief, monarch, ruler.

Aloha (ah-LOH-hah) – love, a form of greeting. On a deeper level, a combination of **alo**—in the presence of—and **ha**—breath, in the sense of Divine Breath or Spirit.

ʻAumakua (au-mah-KOO-ah) – a family or personal god, deified ancestor. Esoteric – the High Self or Superconscious Mind that is aligned with Divinity.

Hauola (hau-OH-lah) – the name of a place of refuge on Kauaʻi. Places of refuge were institutions devoted to forgiveness and spiritual cleansing. A person entering its walls could undergo a purification process to relieve and absolve him of crimes, indiscretions, misdeeds or any imbalance that put him at odds with himself or the world. Hauola is generally translated as *dew of life*, although there are possible connotations suggesting an offering—of life, for life, to life—implying rebirth or renewal.

Hawaiʻi (hah-WHY-ee or Hah-VY-ee) – the largest, easternmost and youngest of the islands that gives its name to the entire chain. On a deeper level, The Divine Breath and Water of Life.

Heiau (hay-au) – a temple or place of worship, a structure devoted to spiritual practice built during the pre-Christian era.

Hikina A Ka Lā (hee-KEE-nah-ah-ka-LAH) – The rising of the sun. The name of a heiau on Kauaʻi.

Honolulu (hoh-noh-LOO-loo) – the capital and largest city of Hawaiʻi, located on Oʻahu island. The name means sheltered bay.

Hoʻoponopono (HOH-oh-POH-noh-POH-noh) – to correct, to make right, to bring into balance. The name given to an ancient problem-solving method focused on forgiveness and restoration of harmony in relationships. Re-envisioned by Morrnah Simeona as an internal process to clean errors within that manifest as problems without.

'Īnea (ee-NEH-ah) – suffering, distress.

Ipo (EE-poh) – sweetheart, lover.

Kahuna (kah-HOO-nah) – an expert in a given profession or activity, roughly the equivalent of a Ph.D. in modern culture. However, unlike the Ph.D., the notion of mastery includes an integrated appreciation and application of the spiritual dimension of the particular domain of expertise. **Kahuna Lapaʻau** (lah-pah-au) – a healer or healing practitioner.

Kāneʻohe (kahh-neh-OH-heh) – the largest city on the windward side of Oʻahu. The legendary meaning, *bamboo husband*, refers to a local woman who compared her husband's cruelty to a bamboo stick.

Kapaʻa (kah-PAH-ah) – solid, sound, steadfast. Name of largest city on Kauaʻi.

Kapu (KAH-poo) – prohibition, restriction, restraint, sacred directive or mandate.

Kauaʻi (kau-AH-ee) – The oldest of the main Hawaiian islands. On a deeper level, the Supreme or Divine Rain. The central mountain of Kauaʻi, Waiʻaleʻale, is the wettest spot on earth, with average rainfall in excess of 400 inches annually. The rain viewed in spiritual terms is the descent of Divine mana.

Kīlauea (kee-lau-AY-ah) – the name of the youngest active volcano on Hawaiʻi island. Also the name of a city on the north shore of Kauaʻi. A kīlau is a type of fern with pervasive underground stems, and also refers to a stalk of the ki (ti) plant used to cast water on an object or person for purposes of purification. Ea refers to life or life-force. On a deeper level, Kīlauea may refer to the life force that comes from sources deep within, bringing to the surface new forms and expressions of the Divine.

Kopa (KOH-pah) – literally, soap. More nuanced—that which cleans, cleanses, removes impurities.

Kupuna (ku-POO-nah) – elder, grandparent, ancestor.

Mahalo (mah-HAH-loh) – Thank you. **Mahalo nui loa** (NOO-ee-LOH-ah) – Thank you very much.

Makahiki (mah-kah-HEE-kee) – a four-month long celebration devoted to the god Lono, beginning around the time of the first rising of the Pleiades star cluster, marking the change from the time of harvest to the new agricultural season.

Maluhia (mah-loo-HEE-ah) – peace, tranquility, inner stillness.

Mana (MAH-nah) – supernatural, spiritual power, force, or energy.

Moloka'i (moh-loh-KAH-ee) – one of the eight main Hawaiian islands, by some accounts harboring the most ancient Hawaiian spiritual consciousness, reported to date back to the pre ali'i times. *Tales From the Night Rainbow* is in part a narrative of a deeply spiritual, communal and non-hierarchical culture that lived on the island prior to the Tahitian migrations circa 1000 AD. Although highly speculative, it is possible that the esoteric spiritual map employed in *Opening the Aloha Mind* and several other books has its origins in the pre-ali'i era.

Nā Pali (NAHH-PAH-lee) – The cliffs, specifically referring to a section of the Kaua'i coast ranging from Polihale Beach to Kē'ē Beach.

O'ahu (oh-AH-hoo) – Most populous of the Hawaiian islands. There is no certain historical meaning of the word, although it has been translated as "the gathering place."

Pōhaku (Pohh-HAH-koo) – stone. Stones are considered as potentially embodying helping spirits and therefore useful to healers and those seeking healing.

Polihale (POH-lee-HAH-leh) – name of beach and beach park on the west coast of Kaua'i. Hale means house, poli means breast or bosom, or, in a more poetic sense, heart. Po refers to night, darkness, or the spirit realm. Other primal cultures have characterized the pre-creation source of all being as the pervasive, undifferentiated darkness or blackness. As such it is akin to the unmanifest unified field which is the ground of creation. Polihale may be seen as the house of the Divine nurturing Source.

Pono (POH-noh) – correct, right, righteous, in balance.

Pumehana (poo-meh-HAH-nah) – warm, warm-hearted.

Puʻuhonua (poo-oo-hoh-NOO-ah) – a place of refuge, or city of refuge. See **Hauola**.

ʻUhane (oo-HAH-neh) – indwelling soul, spirit, ghost. Esoteric – the Middle Self or Conscious Mind.

ʻUnihipili (oo-nee-hee-PEE-lee) – the spirit of a dead person. Esoteric – the Low Self or Subconscious Mind, including basic physiological processes. Sometimes includes the notion of a child-self or inner child.

Waikīkī (why-KEE-KEE or vy-KEE-KEE) – a section of Honolulu best known for its white sand beach. The name means spouting fresh water, a historical reference to streams and wetlands once present in the area.

TO LEARN MORE

The author is a student and practitioner of Hoʻoponopono and this book contains his own understanding of the process. Individuals interested in learning Hoʻoponopono from an authorized teacher are encouraged to attend a class.

Hoʻoponopono is taught world-wide and throughout the year by IZI LLC, the sole authorized sponsor of Self I-Dentity Through Hoʻoponopono® classes. For further information and for scheduled dates and locations, visit http://www.self-i-dentity-through-hooponopono.com

APPENDIX A

Five Questions[5]

The Hoʻoponopono process can be succinctly described in the answers to five defining questions:

1. Who am I?
2. What is a problem?
3. Where is the problem?
4. How can the problem be solved?
5. What is the key?

Who am I?

I am a three-part self—Conscious Mind, Superconscious Mind, Subconscious Mind—created by and joined with Divinity. I am created flawless, an image of the Divine, free, clear, eternal, boundless.

What is a problem?

A problem is memories replaying in Subconscious Mind.

Where is the problem?

The problem is in me.

---

[5] By permission from ʻIhaleakalā Hew Len, Ph.D.

How can the problem be solved?

The problem is solved by the processes of repentance, forgiveness and transmutation, called *cleaning*.

What is the Key?

The Key is our God given I-Dentity. We apply our I-Dentity—The I (Divinity) / Superconscious Mind / Conscious Mind and Subconscious Mind—when we clean. The purpose of life is to use this key to remove the errors (memories) that stand between me and the realization of who I am.

APPENDIX B

Modern Healthcare—an Opportunity to Clean

In modern healing disciplines, technology and technique have triumphed at the expense of human connection—not only the emotional resonance of doctor with patient, but also the doctor's connection to his internal sources of wisdom and knowing.

This situation is alarming but not surprising. Professional psychotherapy, like modern medicine, has become decreasingly guided by its own indigenous evolutionary dynamics, and increasingly defined by external influences with other agendas. The insurance and pharmaceutical industries have no interest in the processes involved in healing, much less in the psychospiritual status of the practitioner. If depression is posited purely as a biochemical imbalance and/or as a consequence of distorted patterns of thinking, and if the criterion for successful treatment is a mere restoration of *functioning,* there is no need for practitioners who, from their own hard-fought self-explorations, can help lead another person to his own unrealized potential. The definition of illness in terms of functional impairment concerns itself, rather, with one's relative inability to perform prescribed roles such as parent, student, or employee. Other factors arguably significant to health such as one's capacity for wisdom, enjoyment, fulfillment, meaning, compassion and equanimity are not explicitly dismissed but rendered incidental when only a handful of sessions are approved for reimbursement.

C.G. Jung pointed out that whenever psyche or culture become one-sided, a compensatory tendency will emerge to restore balance. We can consider the culture of medicine or the culture of psychology in this fashion. When a culture has gone too far down the path of technology, methods that restore human presence to the equation will ascend. When the definition of healing has been reduced to the machine language of mere adequate functionality, methods will emerge that facilitate the human values of internal freedom, joy and clarity. When the practitioner has become defined as nothing more than a vendor of technique, methods will emerge that encourage his own internal freedom, joy and clarity as vital to the healing of anyone he encounters.

The oft-touted double blind experiment so revered by western science is a method that in the healing professions focuses on technique. Is this technique or pill more effective than that technique or pill. What is of less interest is the quality of the presence of the healing practitioner. Does it impact the efficacy of the technique or pill being dispensed? Can we reduce the enterprise to an essential ingredient or is there more to it?

Native traditions have always identified powerful healers or shamans, suggesting that some more than others wield their techniques with greater efficacy. When I was in graduate school there was a debate in the profession about the efficacy of the Rorschach inkblot test, which to many of us missed the whole point. The test is effect-neutral. The mastery of the practitioner is everything. Now the trend is toward computer administered and interpreted questionnaires so naturally the role of the practitioner has been degraded toward a technical function. The depth of understanding of human nature, the cultivation of perceptiveness based on self-exploration and wisdom gained from life experience fade into the background of what have sadly become known as "primitive" methodologies.

This has rendered the landscape of the healing professions barren. While ancient methods and their derivatives may not adapt themselves easily to the double-blind (interesting double meaning) experiment, their continued presence, even their proliferation, suggests that a need of the human spirit to be met on its own terms will not be so easily repressed this time around. Metaphorically, it is perhaps more from the small islands of humanity than from the big continents that the re-visioned formulas for a life that makes sense will call to us.

This era is one of great intellectual and emotional ferment. Old ways are falling, still older ways are re-emerging, and new ways are yet to be fully formed. This is true not only in medicine and psychology but in all areas of knowledge, including economics, philosophy and theology. Ho'oponopono not only provides a problem solving strategy for use by individuals, but in a larger sense its emergence in our time constitutes a balancing, healing force in the world, including the world of healing professions.

PERMISSIONS

Grateful acknowledgement is made to the following publishers and authors for permission to reprint material from their books and media.

Éditions du Seuil, *LES DIRECTIONS DE L'AVENIR Oeuvres XI* by Pierre Teilhard de Chardin ©1973.

'Ihaleakalā Hew Len, Ph.D., the five questions, email communication 09/29/2012

IZI LLC., *Who's In Charge?* by 'Ihaleakalā Hew Len, Ph.D., ©2011

John Wiley & Sons, Inc., *Zero Limits: The Secret Hawaiian System for Wealth, Health, Peace, and More* by Joe Vitale and 'Ihaleakalā Hew Len, Ph.D. ©2007. Reproduced with permission of John Wiley & Sons.

Nā Kāne O Ka Malo Press and Michael Kioni Dudley, Ph.D., *Man, Gods and Nature* ©1990.

Poem (p. 58, Lao Tsu) from TAO TE CHING by Gia-Fu Feng, translation copyright ©1972 by Gia-Fu Feng and Jane English, copyright renewed 2000 by Carol Wilson and Jane English. Used by permission of Alfred A. Knopf, an imprint of the Knopf Doubleday Publishing Group, a division of Random House LLC. All rights reserved. Any third party use of this material, outside of this publication, is prohibited. Interested parties must apply directly to Random House LLC for permission.

Princeton University Press, *The Collected Works of C.G. Jung, Volume 14,* ©1976

www.RadiantArts.com, *Tranceformers: Shamans of the 21ˢᵗ Century* by John Jay Harper ©2006

www.islandmoonlight.com, *Ho'opono: The Hawaiian Way to Put Things Back Into Balance* by Pali Jae Lee ©2006.

SUGGESTED READING

Barnes, Philip K. (1999). *A Concise History of the Hawaiian Islands*. Hilo, Hawai'i: Petroglyph Press.

Bennett, Doug. (2010). *Life and Spirit in the Quantum Field*. Brevard, NC: Take Charge Books.

Bohm, David. (2000). *Wholeness and the Implicate Order*. New York: Routledge.

Beckwith, Martha. (1985). *Hawaiian Mythology*. Honolulu: University of Hawai'i Press.

Bradshaw, John. (1988). *Healing the Shame That Binds You*. Florida: Health Communications, Inc.

Capra, Fritjof. (1975). *The Tao of Physics*. Boston: Shambhala Publications, Inc.

Capra, Fritjof. (1982). *The Turning Point*. New York: Simon & Schuster.

Dudley, Michael Kioni and Agard, Keoni Kealoha. (2003). *A Call for Hawaiian Sovereignty*. Honolulu, Hawai'i: Nā Kāne O Ka Malo Press.

Dudley, Michael Kioni. (1990). *Man, Gods and Nature*. Honolulu, Hawai'i: Nā Kāne O Ka Malo Press.

Fornander, Abraham. *Ancient History of the Hawaiian People*. Honolulu, Hawai'i: Mutual Publishing.

Freud, Sigmund. James Strachey, (Ed.). (1960). *The Ego and the Id*. New York: W.W. Norton & Co.

Grof, Stanislav. (1985). *Beyond the Brain: Birth, Death and Transcendence in Psychotherapy*. Albany, NY: State University of New York Press.

Grof, Stanislav. (1998). *The Cosmic Game*. Albany, NY: State University of New York Press.

Grof, Christina and Grof, Stanislav. (2010). *Holotropic Breathwork*. Albany, NY: State University of New York Press.

Grof, Stanislav. (1988). *The Adventure of Self-Discovery*. New York: State University of New York Press.

Grof, Stanislav and Bennett, Hal Zina. (1992). *The Holotropic Mind*. San Francisco: HarperSanFrancisco.

Grof, Stanislav. (2000). *Psychology of the Future*. Albany, NY: State University of New York Press.

Hall, Lisa Kahaleole. (2005). "Hawaiian at Heart" and Other Fictions. Honolulu: University of Hawai'i Press. *The Contemporary Pacific*. Volume 17, Number 2, 404-413.

Harner, Michael. (1990). *The Way of The Shaman*. San Francisco: Harper & Row.

Harper, John Jay. (2006). *Tranceformers: Shamans of the 21st Century*. Foresthill, CA: Reality Press.

Jung, C.G. (R.F.C. Hull, translator). (1976). *Mysterium Coniunctionis: an Inquiry into the Separation and Synthesis of Psychic Opposites in Psychology and Alchemy*, vol. 14 Bollingen Series XX: The Collected Works of C. G. Jung, 2d edition. Princeton, NJ: Princeton University Press.

Kafatos, Menas and Nadeau, Robert. (1990). *The Conscious Universe*. New York: Springer-Verlag.

Katz, Mabel. (2009). *The Easiest Way*. Woodland Hills, CA: Your Business Press.

Kuhn, Thomas. (1962). *The Structure of Scientific Revolutions*. Chicago: The University of Chicago Press.

Laszlo, Ervin. (2008). *Quantum Shift in the Global Brain*. Rochester, VT: Inner Traditions.

Liliuokalani. (1964). *Hawaii's Story by Hawaii's Queen*. Tokyo, Japan: Charles E. Tuttle Company, Inc.

Long, Max Freedom. (1976*). The Secret Science Behind Miracles*. Marina Del Ray, CA: DeVorss & Company.

Maslow, Abraham. (1976). *The Farther Reaches of Human Nature*. New York: Penguin/Arkana.

McTaggart, Lynn. (2003). *The Field: The Quest for the Secret Force of the Universe*. New York: Harper Collins.

Nørretranders, Tor. (1991). *The User Illusion*. New York: Penguin Books.

Nourse, James C. (2008). *Simple Spirituality: Finding Your Own Way*. Hendersonville, NC: City of Refuge Books.

O'Keefe, Edward M. (2012). *Take It From the Top: What To Do with a Peak Experience*.

Pukui, Mary Kawena and Elbert, Samuel H. (1986). *Hawaiian Dictionary*. Honolulu: University of Hawaii Press.

Twigg-Smith, Thurston. (1998). *Hawaiian Sovereignty: Do the Facts Matter?* Honolulu: Goodale Publishing.

Vitale, Joe and Hew Len, 'Ihaleakalā. (2007). *Zero Limits: The Secret Hawaiian System for Wealth, Health, Peace and More*. Hoboken, NJ: John Wiley & Sons, Inc.

Wesselman, Hank. (2011). *The Bowl of Light*. Boulder, CO. SoundsTrue.

Willis, Koko and Lee, Pali Jae. (1990). *Tales From the Night Rainbow*. Honolulu: Night Rainbow Publishing Co.

ABOUT THE AUTHOR

Jim Nourse, Ph.D., L.Ac. practices clinical psychology and classical Chinese medicine at the Center for Integrated Health and Healing in Brevard, North Carolina. His 40 years in the health care field have been driven by a passion for the application of ancient and transpersonal approaches to problems faced by modern people. He began learning the Self I-dentity Through Ho'oponopono® process in 2006 and considers it central to his life and work. He lives in Hendersonville, North Carolina with his wife Judith—reflexologist, Feng Shui consultant and companion on roads less-traveled. He may be contacted through his website: www.jamesnourse.com.

ʻĀmama, ua noa, lele wale
The kapu is lifted. The words fly free . . .

Made in the USA
Las Vegas, NV
21 June 2022

50532000R00100